Becoming the Mom I Wish I'd Had

Sylvy,

You are. an awesome woman & mother that I am honored to count as a friend.

I wish you joy & prosperity in ABUNDANCE!

— Ve——

love Ver

PRAISES

For the book, *Becoming the Mom I Wish I'd Had...*

This book is full of practical wisdom for anyone wishing to be the best parent that you can be. If you want emotionally healthy, creative, confident, loving, responsible children, buy this book and heed Venus Taylor's sage advice. I am recommending it to every parent I know.

Susan Campbell, Ph.D.
Author of Getting Real, Saying What's Real, and
The Couples Journey
www.susancampbell.com

I can't put the book...down.

[It] is a MUST read for every mom and future mom. Even those who have not come from abusive homes, repeat patterns that their parents did, etc.

It really makes you mindful of how we parent, and conscious of how important our job of mom really is.

S. Resnicoff
Lakewood, NJ

[This] book has touched my heart so deeply.

I've been lamenting the gulf between my desire to have close relationships with my children, and the reality of the distance that some of my shortcomings create.

Your book is such a compassionate, wise and practical response to this chasm. I am continuing to work through the exercises...

I think that it will be well-appreciated by parents in all stages of the child-rearing journey.

J. James-Carnes
New London, CT

For Venus Taylor, Founder of The Family Healing Institute...

Venus has allowed me to see things within myself in a gentle nonthreatening way. Interacting with her has allowed me to have more patience with my children and to allow them to be who they are.

N. Muhammad
Boston, MA

Her compassion, devotion to family and generous nature will help support...families in a crisis... [or just] in need of a friend and counselor.

L. Mitchell
Roxbury, MA

Venus has the ability to listen beneath the words and hear what is being felt as well as expressed. She has the courage to share what she has gleaned and gently push one to action.

A. James-Curtis
Flossmoor, IL

[Venus] is very insightful and knowledgeable in all areas applicable to coaching, relationships, success, abundance and personal empowerment.

We all create our 'stories' which can keep us stuck in repeating patterns.

Venus can help you get to the bottom of your 'story' so you can become who it is you are really wanting to be, and thus achieve your highest goals.

R. Reid
Arlington, MA

Becoming the Mom I Wish I'd Had

How to Heal Yourself and Your Family Through HEART-Based Parenting

Venus Taylor, Ed.M.

Lower Mills Publishing Company
Dorchester, Massachusetts

Author portrait by Carol Lundeen
Cover design by Vaughan Davidson

Published by Lower Mills Publishing Company
www.lowermillspublishing.com

Publisher's Cataloging-in-Publication
(Provided by Quality Books, Inc.)

Taylor, Venus.
    Becoming the mom I wish I'd had : how to heal
yourself and your family through heart-based parenting /
Venus Taylor. -- 1st ed.
    p. cm.
    LCCN 2009901874
    ISBN-13: 978-0-9823186-0-7
    ISBN-10: 0-9823186-0-X
    ISBN-13: 978-0-9823186-1-4
    ISBN-10: 0-9823186-1-8
    [etc.]

    1. Mother and child. 2. Parenting.   I. Title.

HQ755.85.T39 2009   306.874'3
                           QBI09-600015

www.HealMyFamily.com
venus@HealMyFamily.com

First Edition, March 2009
ISBN 978-0-9823186-0-7 (Paperback)
ISBN 978-0-9823186-1-4 (Audio CD)
ISBN 978-0-9823186-2-1 (Digital Download/Ebook)
ISBN 978-0-9823186-3-8 (Audio Download)

10 9 8 7 6 5 4 3 2 1

~ TABLE OF CONTENTS ~

~ ACKNOWLEDGEMENTS ~

All my love and thanks to my best friend and husband, Hycel III, and my two awesome children, Jasmine and Buddy, for your patience and support.

Thanks also to my mastermind team – Laurie, Janette, Sari, Fran, Denise, and Breindy. You were the doulas, the midwives, that helped this baby to be born. Thanks for embracing me with your encouragement and helping me hold myself accountable.

And also, thanks to my mentors, Dr. Susan Campbell (author of *Saying What's Real*) and Diana Haskins Sterling (author of *Parent as Coach*), for inspiring me and adding skills to my passion.

~ A NOTE TO READERS ~

Some of the stories that follow are sad, and may be difficult to read.

I share them with you because they are true, and they illustrate that any pain suffered during the course of a life can be healed.

Please know that I have nothing but love for anyone mentioned in this book.

I have long since forgiven anyone who has ever brought pain into my life experience; and, in fact, I have moved from forgiveness to gratitude.

I am so grateful for everything in my life today – including my wonderful husband and incredible children – that whatever it took to get me to this point, I fully appreciate. I do not begrudge any of it.

My love and hugs to you who may uncover memories of your own pain while reading this book.

Let's celebrate, together, our victory over any harm that has ever come to us.

We have survived.

We were not destroyed.

Nothing ever could destroy us.

Every experience – even a painful one – contains a lesson. When we learn the lesson, we can feel enriched, rather than diminished, by the experience.

Even if all we learn is never to do to others what was done to us – then the experience teaches us to make the world a better place.

We heal ourselves by healing the world, and vice versa. And we heal the world by healing our families.

Becoming the Mom I Wish I'd Had is about transforming a Legacy of Pain into a Legacy of Healing through the act of mindful, conscious, HEART-Based Parenting.

I hope you enjoy the book, and the journey.

With love and gratitude, Venus

~ INTRODUCTION ~

If you are, or soon will be, a mother, and your heart is set on becoming the best mother you can possibly be...this book is for you.

If you've had a less-than-perfect relationship with your own mother... if you were abused, neglected, abandoned...and desire a close, loving relationship with your children unlike any you've ever seen...then this book is *especially* for you.

This book is about healing.

It is about the power you have to heal yourself and your family, through the choices you make as a parent.

Many of us, for whatever reason, do not wish to parent our children the way we were parented. It's practically the Universal Parenting Creed: To do better with our kids than was done with us.

This is especially true if your childhood was less than ideal. Those of us who were hurt as children – neglected, abandoned, or abused – or who carry any "baggage" from our relationship with our parents, often want very much to hand down to our children a different legacy than we inherited.

And we can.

In this book, we will walk through the process of transforming our Emotional Baggage into a Treasure Chest of Parenting Wisdom. We will put the past to work, letting it teach us everything it can about how to become the best parents we can be.

We will learn how to heal ourselves and our family line by exercising the 3 Fundamental Principles of HEART-Based Parenting. We will learn what it means to create a Legacy of Healing, and to end the Legacy of Pain.

We will stock our parenting toolkit with the 9 Tools of the HEART-Based Parenting approach. And we'll learn how to use these tools to *inspire* good behavior instead of *enforcing* it – ensuring a close, loving, respectful relationship with our kids

In the end, we will create a home where parents and children feel respected, seen, heard, valued, and invited to be their best, most authentic self.

The HEART-Based Parenting approach, which you'll learn more about later, is a culmination of 40 years of experience.

Some of what you'll read was learned during my Master of Education Program at Harvard University. I studied Risk and Prevention before working as a Prevention Specialist with teens in the Boston Public School system.

Some of it was learned through my training as a Certified Family Coach. And from the families I have assisted in their efforts to heal emotional wounds and stay connected.

The core of my parenting education, however, came from my own troubled childhood, and my efforts to secure a better life experience for my children.

You'll learn more as you continue reading, but I wanted to take a moment to introduce myself, in case you're wondering, *Who are you, and why should I trust you?*

I was one of those kids who realized at a very young age, that the only person I could trust to look out for my best interest was Me.

At age 4, I began to be molested, routinely, by my step-father.

I wanted it to stop. But I was too afraid to tell my mother directly. I'd seen my mother cry numerous times. I didn't want to tell her something that would bring her more pain.

Also, I was scared of getting beaten if she didn't believe me. I was spanked for every error. But for "lying," Mom would beat me until she was exhausted. Once, so severely that the belt broke the skin. So, until I could find the words to convince her I was telling the truth, I didn't dare try.

So, instead of telling my mother directly, I dropped hints, hoping she would catch on to what was happening.

Once, I wrote all the sex-related swear words I knew on the bathroom wall at home. Often, I walked around the house with my pajamas twisted backwards the way my step-father had left them the night before.

I even told babysitters, hoping they would tell my mother for me. But, both times I tried that, the babysitters took advantage and had me "show" them what I was talking about, using their bodies and mine. So, I gave up on that idea.

When I turned 8, and it looked like my mother was divorcing my step-father for other reasons, I took a chance, and told her how he had been abusing me. I figured, since they were already breaking up, my story would only add to her pain, not cause it.

My step-father denied it. He said I was lying.

I looked at my mother, who seemed to be hurting so badly that I wanted to do whatever I could to help her.

So I took it back.

They reconciled. The abuse continued.

I told my mother again, once a year, every year, and the same scene repeated. He denied it. Mom believed him.

I never took it back, though, after that first time.

I simply realized that I was on my own. My mother wouldn't protect me.

Finally, at age 11, when I couldn't take it anymore, I told my church pastor. Then I told my mother that I had told the pastor. The abuse finally ended.

My mother divorced my step-father after warning me that life would be financially difficult after he left.

I assured her I could handle being poor if it meant not being molested anymore.

I only shared this sad story to illustrate how completely alone I felt as a child.

The sexual abuse from my step-father, the physical abuse from my mother, and the extreme poverty we suffered as Mom struggled to raise four children on her own, convinced me that I had no one but myself to depend on.

Such a realization at such a young age can take a person's life in one of two directions: Determination or Despair.

I chose determination. I chose to be strong enough to endure anything life threw at me.

Through faith and focus, I held tight to the reins of my life and charged steadily forward on a path of success.

I completed high school by age 17, college by age 21. I graduated college already married to the man of my dreams. I was happy and grateful for all I had overcome.

However, five years into my marriage, when I was pregnant with our first child, I got scared. I wondered, *What kind of mother will I be?*

I wanted my children to have a much different childhood from the one I'd had.

I wanted my kids to feel loved and respected. I wanted them to feel ownership of their bodies, minds, and destinies.

I wanted kids who would do what's right based on their personal desire to be good, not based on fear of punishment.

And most of all, I wanted kids who would feel connected to me and to their father. I wanted them to feel safe and secure, not alienated and alone.

That meant I would have to be a much different kind of mother than the one I'd had.

This book describes how I learned to parent in such a way that I not only furthered my personal healing, but also created a Legacy of Healing, and wrote a new chapter in my family's history.

The book is written in two parts.

Part 1: Looking Back, is a journey back through childhood. We'll use a 3 step process called *Trial-to-Treasure*, that will help us squeeze every ounce of parenting wisdom from our happiest and most painful childhood memories. This process infuses our parenting with a level of empathy that will keep us forever attuned to the needs of children.

In *Part II: Looking Forward*, we will examine the 3 Fundamental Beliefs and 9 Parenting Tools that are essential to the HEART-Based Parenting approach.

It is my hope that whether you are working to heal a painful family legacy, or simply striving to improve your parenting skills...whether you are expecting a newborn or looking to restore a deep connection with your teenager…that you will find insights here that will help you become the parent you want to be.

I would love to hear your comments and experiences with this material. Please share your comments, suggestions, feedback, wins, at venus@HealMyFamily.com. Thank you.

Let's begin our journey…

~ Part I ~

Looking Back:

Putting The Past

To Work For You

Chapter 1

Exploring Your Mom's Mistakes

The scariest gift I ever received came during the 17th week of my first pregnancy. It was an ultrasound picture, showing a little 5-inch creature growing inside me, with arms and legs, a beating heart ... and the face of my mother.

I happen to have very mixed feelings about my mother. I love her dearly, but it wasn't an accident that I chose to live 1100 miles away from her. Our relationship is complicated. The distance helps us get along better.

So you can imagine how upset I was to see her here in Boston, inside my body, instead of in Chicago where she belonged.

In shock, I shrank away from the doctor's office that day, with a voice in my head repeating, *I'm giving birth to my mother...I'm giving birth to my mother...What does this mean?*

By the time I made it home on the subway that day, I fearfully trembled with a new thought: *Besides Mom's face, what else might this child inherit from me?*

It was scary enough that my daughter was inheriting my mother's face – which is also my face, whether I want to admit it or not. What scared me even more, was the possibility that if I made the same mistakes my mother did – if I parented with a lot of spanking, and emotional distance – my daughter might inherit my Baggage.

You know what Baggage is: That heavy load of painful memories that seem to define us and our relationships. Those stories from childhood that we pull out as evidence of why we keep having painful relationships, why we don't like ourselves or our bodies, why we can't live our dreams the way luckier people can.

I couldn't control the face thing, but I was determined not to hand down the Baggage. I wasn't sure how, but I was committed to discovering or inventing a way to raise my child with tenderness and closeness, to instill self-discipline without violence, to raise a happy, confident, person who enjoyed a healthy, close relationship with me and her father.

.

I believed in the adage: Those who do not study their history are doomed to repeat it.

So, to avoid repeating history – to avoid handing down the legacy of pain I had inherited – I decided to study it.

At the risk of falling into depression, I dug down deep into my history, my baggage.

I let my baggage teach me everything it could about how to become the mother I most wanted to be for my children.

I sorted and sifted through the dark, painful memories I had lugged around all my life – the physical and emotional abuse by a well-intentioned mother, the years of sexual abuse by a psychotic step-father.

However, I was looking for something different than usual.

Instead of excuses, rationalizations, blame, and guilt that I usually uncovered from my "Baggage of Trials," this time I scanned the memories for something useful. Something that would help me build a better tomorrow, not keep me repeating yesterday.

What I found was a bounty of mothering wisdom. A guide for what to do, and what not to do, as a mother.

There were lessons to be learned in those memories I carried. Lessons about the importance of empathy in parenting. About keeping lines of communication open so painful secrets can't hide. And how to stay close with kids so they don't feel alone in the world.

Finding these golden nuggets of parenting wisdom turned my Baggage of Trials into a Treasure Chest of Parenting Wisdom.

It is this Trial-to-Treasure process, that we will explore now. The 3 steps are as follows:

1. Revisit the Memory
2. Acknowledge the Effects
3. Uncover the Treasure

We will journey through the past and zoom into childhood memories – the painful ones, as well as the happy ones. We will remember what built us up as a child, and what tore us down.

In the process, we will gain insights that will help us to be the most empathic, effective parents we can be.

Let's cover the painful memories in this chapter. We'll enjoy the happier memories in Chapter 2.

Trial-to-Treasure Step 1: Revisit the Memory

First, we'll unpack the baggage one story at a time. You may want to go to a quiet, private space. Take a journal or a voice recorder – or a close friend if you like – and **jot down your answers and observations.**

If it's too painful to go back in first person, try seeing each scene as if it's happening to someone else. Watch the movie of what happened as if through a camera lens. You can zoom in or zoom way out based on how safe you feel reviewing the film.

❖ ❖ ❖ ❖ ❖ ❖ ❖ ❖ ❖ ❖ ❖ ❖ ❖ ❖ ❖

Exercise 1.1: Revisit the Painful Memory

1. Examine the painful memory you retell most often. Do your best to actually see, in your mind's eye, what happened. Look at the little girl that was you. What's happening to her in this scene? How is she feeling? If she could say what she really wants to say, what would it be?

2. If you're feeling safe enough, take a deep breath, exhale slowly, and see if you can BE that girl in the scene. Count backwards from 10 to 1 as you step back in time and into the experience of the little girl. Feel what she's feeling as if it were happening right now. Stay there. Don't rush to come out of it. Take your time and feel it fully.

3. Say what that little girl wants to say. Say what she's feeling. Say what she's thinking. Say what she wants. You're bigger now. You can say now what you couldn't say then. If you're

alone or with a safe friend, speak out loud. If you don't have enough privacy, speak softly or write it down.

4. Before leaving the memory, comfort the little girl as you leave her behind. Wrap your arms around yourself, or hug your face with your hands, while you remind the little girl in you that it's all okay now.

5. Take a deep breath, count forward from 1 to 10 as you bring your awareness back to the present.

This reflective exercise provides at least two benefits.

The first is **Empathy for Our Children.** Seeing life again through the eyes of a child, remembering our childhood feelings and thoughts, puts us in touch with how children experience life. This helps us to be more mindful of what we say and do, because we're conscious of how they might experience our actions.

The second benefit of the above exercise is **Empathy for Ourselves.** This exercise isn't about wallowing in self-pity, or blaming others. It is about honoring how far we've come. And celebrating our gratitude to the spiritual and physical forces that helped us survive.

Empathy is the first and most important of the 9 tools in the HEART-Based Parenting toolkit. We'll discuss it more in Part II of the book.

Now that we've revisited the painful memory, let's acknowledge its meaning in our lives so far.

Trial-to-Treasure Step 2: Acknowledge the Effect

Once we've drained some of the pain out of our memories, we can look at them more objectively.

Before we uncover the lesson this memory teaches us today, let's acknowledge how this memory has shaped us until now.

❖ ❖ ❖ ❖ ❖ ❖ ❖ ❖ ❖ ❖ ❖ ❖ ❖ ❖ ❖

Exercise 1.2: Acknowledge How Events Shaped You

1. For each event, summarize what you learned about **yourself** AT THE TIME of the event. What thoughts about yourself were planted in your head as a result of this experience? What feelings did you begin to hold about yourself during the event?

2. For each event, summarize what you learned about **others** AT THE TIME of the event. What did you think about the specific person or people involved? What ideas formed about what people (parents, grownups, men, women) are like? What feelings did you begin to hold about people like that?

3. For each event, summarize what you learned about the way the **world** works AT THE TIME of the event. What did this event teach you about "the way things are," or "the way life is?" How did this event shape your feelings about life, or about the world?

❖ ❖ ❖ ❖ ❖ ❖ ❖ ❖ ❖ ❖ ❖ ❖ ❖ ❖ ❖

Like the previous exercise, this one sharpens our sense of empathy for ourselves and for our children.

Negative, limiting beliefs we hold about ourselves, others, and life in general are most likely based on painful events that happened in the past. Our beliefs are not "Truth." They are explanations our child-brains created to explain why things were happening to us.

As grownups, remembering the childhood events that shaped our beliefs, we are now free to re-interpret the assumptions we made back then, and to let go of the beliefs that keep us from moving forward.

For example, I realized that, as an adult, I harbored the belief that unless I went along (or appeared to go along) with what others wanted, they wouldn't love me. I believed that the *real* me was unlovable.

This, of course, led to a lot of passive-aggressive behavior. I would hide, ignore, and lie about my true feelings; I would pretend to agree with things, and then just not follow through. It made relationships difficult, to say the least.

I traced the belief that I was "unlovable" back to the times when I was spanked for expressing my individuality. Adults called me "stubborn" and "hard-headed."

Eventually I learned to keep my feelings and opinions to myself. To blend in, so I wouldn't be punished.

Revisiting these events showed me that my unlovable-ness was not "Truth." It was simply a conclusion I came to based on what happened. There are a dozen other ways to explain what happened.

Maybe the adults in my life were stressed out didn't want to deal with my resistance. Who knows? Who cares?

Acknowledging that my unlovable-ness was not "Truth," freed me to find new ways to express myself fully in my life.

That is how this work heals both us and our families. We get to re-parent ourselves as we determine the kind of parents we want to be for our children.

We get to heal our wounds as we learn not to inflict similar wounds on our kids.

As we acknowledge the effects of others' insensitivity, we consciously decide to be more sensitive parents.

This takes us to the final step: Uncovering the Treasure.

Trial-to-Treasure Step 3: Uncover the Treasure

Let's comb through the memories one last time. This time, from our present-day perspective as mothers. What do these memories teach us that we can use today?

Exercise 1.3: Uncovering the Treasure of Parenting Wisdom

Reviewing each event one last time, ask the following questions:

1. What did I need most when this event was happening? What does this teach me about what kids need? How can I be sure my kid gets what he/she needs?

2. Who was there for me to turn to back then? Who would listen? How can I ensure my child feels seen and heard? What kind of relationships are important for my child to have – with me and with others?

3. What did I want most back then? How can I learn and supply what's most important to my child?

4. What are some of the indirect ways I tried to communicate my pain back then? How can I stay tuned into my child so I can understand his/her indirect ways of telling me something important?

5. How valued/cherished did I feel? What are some ways to ensure my child feels valued and loved?

This final step is, I believe, the only good reason to hold on to and reflect on the past.

The past is over. It is done. It is only our choice to focus on it that keeps it alive in us.

We can be whomever we choose from this day forward. The past does not dictate the future.

The only good purpose the past can serve is to help us create a better present and future.

By delving into our memories and learning true empathy for our children, we transform pain into promise.

We heal ourselves by gaining a deeper understanding of who we've been, and a better sense of who we wish to become.

We heal our families by consciously deciding how we will interact with them. By being aware of the potential effects of our words and deeds. And by honoring their point of view.

Learning from the Past

It's fitting that we call painful memories and their effects on us, "Baggage."

Our Baggage can be a heavy weight that slows us down and holds us back. It can become the excuse for why we can't move forward in our lives.

Using the Trial-to-Treasure process to sift through the baggage and toss out the dead weight (blame, excuses, guilt, what we wish had been), lightens the load.

What's left is simply "What Happened" or "What Was." And by studying what was, using the Trial-to-Treasure process, we can learn lessons from the past that help us create a better future.

In the end, instead of a Baggage of Trials – to lug around, and hand down to our children – we'll have uncovered a Treasure Chest of Parenting Wisdom, filled with golden nuggets of Lessons Learned.

Our kids will inherit this treasure chest, rather than the baggage. We will create a legacy of healing in our family line, rather than continuing a legacy of pain.

For review, the 3 steps of the Trial-to-Treasure process are as follows:

Step 1: Revisit (and re-experience) the memory

Step 2: Acknowledge the effects

Step 3: Uncover the Treasure

This process works with happy memories, as well as painful ones.

Now that we've exhausted the painful memories, and learned many good parenting lessons from them, let's look at the happy memories. There is much to be learned there as well.

Chapter 2

Celebrating What Your Mom Did Well

It shouldn't surprise you to know that, despite the choices she made that brought me pain, I love my mother very much.

In fact, the good she did outweighed the bad, which is, I believe, why we still have a loving relationship today (well, that, plus the 1100-mile buffer).

After sorting through the sad scenes of my childhood, I noticed that, without effort, all the wonderful things my mother did to show her deep, powerful love for me came flooding into my memory.

It was like I could see and feel the beautiful memories of my mother, once the ugly ones were out of the way.

I noticed that much of what I love most about myself came from my mother.

My love of education, for instance, came directly from her. She taught me to read when I was 3 years old. She pulled strings for me to get admitted to 1st grade before I'd reached the age cutoff. And she always advocated for me to have the best education she could afford.

She always saw me as smart. Capable. And that's a huge part of my identity today.

It was one of the many strengths she lovingly instilled in me.

I decided to capture happy memories like these and dissect them just as I had done with the sad ones.

I wanted to understand what made them so powerful. What did I gain from them?

What was really happening during the happiest scenes of my life that made me stand tall and feel loved?

Because, more than anything, I wanted to hand down these feelings to my children, as well.

Ironically, the Trial-to-Treasure process that helped me squeeze so much wisdom from my painful memories, worked just as well with the joyful ones.

Using the Trial-to-Treasure process on happy memories helped me understand what to say and do with my children that would help them develop their strengths, feel loved and valued, and express themselves confidently.

Exploring the Good Memories

Chances are, no matter what mom did wrong, she did at least some things right. She baked good cookies or made a big deal out of celebrating your birthday. She taught you skills that you still use today.

Perhaps, like my mother, yours did her best to overcome her own painful childhood and provided a life for you that was better than what she'd experienced.

Hopefully there is at least one thing you can look back and say that Mom did well.

However, I have a friend who tries and tries and cannot thing of one nice thing to say about her mother.

If this is you, complete the following exercises anyway, thinking of other people who were in your life as a child. Perhaps the good memories were with your grandmother, or aunt. Maybe it was your dad, or uncle.

"One person is all it takes." That's what I remember most from my Master of Education Program at the Harvard University School of Education. I studied Risk and Prevention, and the evidence showed that what keeps a kid from succumbing to complete despair during a harsh childhood is having **one person** who believes in her.

One person who has high expectations for a child, who sees and reflects the good in that child, can save her from a complete lack of belief in herself.

Who was there for you?

Was your childhood mostly sunny, with just a few clouds? Or were there just a few rays of sun to break up the dark monotony?

Either way, let's zoom in on the bright spots. Let's complete our understanding of "what works," so we can bring the light into our children's lives.

This journey into the good memories can also remind us that **we don't have to do the work of parenting all by ourselves**. The more people confirming and reflecting a child's goodness, the better.

So, as we think about the good Mom did, and the joy others brought to our childhood experience, let's be mindful of how important it is for our children to have other mentors, besides us, who will help them learn to know and love themselves.

Step 1: Revisit the Memory

When you think back to the times in your childhood when you were happiest, what memories come up first? What was happening when your smile was the biggest? Who was there and what did they do to make this event so memorable?

Whether the memory is a specific event, or an aspect of your childhood that was handled well, go into that experience and see how much it can teach you about what is important to do with your children.

❖ ❖ ❖ ❖ ❖ ❖ ❖ ❖ ❖ ❖ ❖ ❖ ❖ ❖ ❖
Exercise 2.1: Revisit the Joyful Memory

What's the first happy scene that comes to mind when you remember your childhood fondly? What did your mom, or another, do that you especially liked?

Go back to that time. Step into that memory. Really give yourself a chance to be back there and enjoy it as if it is happening again, right now.

While you're there, pull out your journal or voice recorder, or telephone a close friend, and answer the following questions:

1. Count backwards from 10 to 1, and as you do, slip further out of this time and deeper into the memory.

    BE in that scene. What is happening? What do you see? What do you smell? Taste? Hear? What do you feel on your skin? Describe every detail you can remember.

2. What are you feeling in your heart? What are you thinking in your head – is it words? Is it pictures? Speak aloud, or write down, every word or image that represents what you're feeling in this memory. Say whatever comes to mind, don't over-analyze it.

3. If it feels right, hug yourself tight and celebrate this good experience.

4. Take a deep breath, count forward from 1 to 10 as you bring your awareness back to the present.

Wasn't that fun?

Do you notice the difference between how you feel after revisiting a happy memory and how you feel after revisiting a painful memory?

Remembering the good brings on such a rush of pleasure, we could probably use good memories as "drugs." When you're feeling bad, conjure up a good memory. Escape into it. Bring that joy into your spirit and share it liberally with others.

Repeat this exercise exploring at least half as many happy memories as the painful ones you examined earlier.

If possible, try to revisit even *more* happy memories than you did painful ones.

As mentioned earlier, these joyful memories could be specific events, like the time your mom stood up for you against misguided teacher. Or it could be parenting choices your mom made that you recognize had a good effect on you, like making sure you had your own room, or handling sibling disputes fairly.

Again, if mom didn't have one single redeeming quality – which would be extremely rare –think of other positive people or events that crossed your path. Was school the place you felt most rewarded? Was it a sport or a coach that brought out the best in you?

Remembering the people and events that brought us joy as children can remind us how important it is for our children to have great, loving experiences to grow on.

Step 2: Acknowledge the Effect

Now, as you did with the painful memories, go back into each scene or event listed. Explain what they did for you, how they added to you as a person. What did these memories teach you about yourself? About others? About the world?

Exercise 2.2: How Joyful Experiences Shaped You

1. For each event, summarize what you learned about **yourself** AT THE TIME of the event. What thoughts about yourself were planted in your head as a result of this experience? What feelings did you begin to hold about yourself during the event?

2. For each event, summarize what you learned about **others** AT THE TIME of the event. What did you think about the specific person or people involved? What ideas formed about what people (parents, grownups, men, women) are like? What feelings did you begin to hold about people like that?

3. For each event, summarize what you learned about the way the **world** works AT THE TIME of the event. What did this event teach you about "the way things are," or "the way life is?" How did this event shape your feelings about life, or about the world?

The exercise above is identical to Exercise 1.2, for our positive experiences shape us as surely as our negative ones.

Sometimes we seem to notice more readily the marks left by life's beatings than the indentations left by life's hugs.

Look at who you are. Your beauty. Your strength. The things you do best. The parts of your personality that you love most.

They developed not only *in spite* of your childhood, but were inspired by some of your most favorite, cherished childhood experiences.

Step 3: Uncover the Treasure

Finally, review your positive childhood experiences with the eyes of a mother. Learn every delicious insight you'd like to bring into your relationship with your child.

Exercise 2.3: Learning What To Do As A Mother

Reviewing each event one last time, ask the following questions:

1. What did I enjoy most about this event or decision? What does this teach me about the significance of joy and pleasure in my child's life?

2. What was so special about this event that it stayed with me this long? How might I help my child develop good memories that last a lifetime? How might I help him develop good memories that speak louder to him than any painful ones?

3. What does this memory remind me about what I find "fun?" How do I arrange to have "fun" these days? Am I having enough fun? Could there be more? How can I fulfill my desire for fun in my life – both with and without my children?

4. With whom did I have the most fun as a kid? What was it about this person made them so much fun to be with? How might I bring a similar quality into my relationship with my child? How will my child remember me as "fun?"

There's no such thing as a childhood with too much laughter.

While we want our kids to be competent, disciplined, and responsible – we also want them to be happy.

Let's remember how great a role we play in bringing joy into our children's lives.

Let's be mindful of how we can use our words and actions to help our children feel cherished and capable.

Expose them to others who love them well, so they learn how immensely lovable they are.

Fostering healthy, happy relationships with our children will help them to develop equally healthy, happy relationships with others.

That may be the most important life skill of all.

Honoring the Good

During the time that I was brooding over my painful childhood memories, I didn't call my mother very often.

I was angry. I was sad. I didn't want to talk to her. And if I did, it was to let her know how upset I was.

Once the clouds cleared away, and I bathed in the sunshine of my favorite memories of Mom, I eagerly expressed my love for her.

I made a list of the things I most appreciated about my mom. And for several years I sent her a Thank You note, honoring one thing about her, each Mother's Day.

Celebrating the good that mom had done, felt as healing for me as it did for her.

Spending as much (or more) time remembering the good as we do remembering the bad is the key to healing relationships.

Our relationships say a lot about us: The healthier they are, the healthier we are.

The healthier we are, the better moms we can be.

Chapter 3

Forgiving Mom, Healing Yourself

By the time we reach our teens - if not sooner - we often begin to realize our parents aren't perfect. Some of their choices don't make sense - not just to us as children, but in the grand scheme of things.

I remember at age 12, making a sincere effort to save my relationship with my mother. I could feel myself growing to resent her. I noticed that, as I got older, I saw her more as an obstacle in my life and less as an ally.

At 12, I felt that the first thing that would make our relationship better, that would keep me from growing more distant from her, was if she would stop spanking me.

The spankings (or whippings, as we called them) didn't make me respect her or her rules. They made her seem ridiculous to me. They made me feel like I hated her. They filled me with thoughts like, "How soon can I grow up and get out of here?"

But I wanted to feel close to her. I wanted a mom I could talk to and trust. I didn't want to feel alone for the rest of the years I had to be a kid. So, I made one daring attempt to take our relationship to a more dignified level.

After rehearsing the speech in my room, I found Mom at the kitchen table, sewing buttons on a shirt sleeve. I told her I had something I wanted to talk with her about.

She looked at me with love and concern, placed her sewing down on her lap, and said, "I'm listening."

Then, with all the maturity I could muster, I asked, "Mom, you know how you're always saying how 'mature' I am...well, I think I'm getting too mature for whippings.

"I've been wondering if you could find another way to teach me a lesson when I do something wrong? 'Cause I don't think whipping me is doing what you want it to do.

"I don't learn to stop disobeying, I just learn how to try harder not to get caught. And I don't feel bad for what I did, I just feel angry at you. And really distant from you.

"So, I was thinking, if you could give me a 'talking to,' or ground me, or something else, I'd probably learn from that better than a spanking."

I trembled nervously, and looked at her, hoping that my fantasy would come true: *She'll ask me to pull up a chair, and thank me for being so brave. Then she'll say, "OK, let's talk about this and find something that works." And I'll finally feel like we have a real relationship.*

Instead, I watched as the laughter she tried to contain came bursting through her pinched lips.

"Oh, you're too 'mature' for whippings, huh?" she laughed. "That's a good one. Well, I say, 'Obedience is better than sacrifice.' If you don't want a whipping, then you should act right."

She ended with, "I'm the mother. And as long as you live in my house, you're gonna get a whipping if you disobey. Period."

I felt humiliated, and terribly sad. I returned to my room, knowing that there was no room for growth in our relationship. I lost all hope that I would ever feel connected to her.

That day, I began calling her "Mother" instead of "Mom." It seemed to fit her rigidity. It indicated the role was choosing to play instead of developing real relationship with me. It was also my way of signifying that there was no more tenderness in my heart for her.

As an adult, I can look back and see that, as insensitive as she was, my mother did not mean any harm, really. She honestly thought she was doing the right thing.

She had been taught, "If you spare the rod, you spoil the child," and she was not about to let me be spoiled.

She believed it was her duty and her right to whip children until they were old enough to leave home. (I believe I got my last whipping at age 13.)

It's not that she was right and I was wrong. She was simply acting out of what she understood to be true – and she was not of a mind to let a 10 year old teach her how to be a mother.

Moms are People, Too

Newsflash: Moms can be wrong. Moms are human. Moms are fallible. **Moms make mistakes.**

Their actions are based on their personal history, their cultural and religious beliefs, and sometimes the latest trends in childrearing.

Moms can be well-intentioned, yet mis-directed.

Sadly, since our moms (and dads) make up such a big part of our worlds as children, their minor missteps can bring us major pain.

Who mom is can affect who we become.

The good news is this: Although the past may have affected who we *have* become, **the past has no hold whatsoever on who we *can* become.**

The Trial-to-Treasure process, and the HEART-Based Parenting Approach we'll discuss in Part II, help us to become the people we want to be, so we can be the parents our children deserve.

Before we leave the past and focus on the future, let's briefly address the importance of Forgiveness.

Forgive Mom as You Wish to Be Forgiven

Since you're reading this book, I assume you have joined the "Sorority of Motherhood," or you soon will.

I invite you to bring to the "Sorority" the spirit of forgiveness that you'd like to find there as *you* muddle through it.

Remember, every mom does the best she knows how to do at the time. You don't have to agree that your mom did "the best she could." But given her circumstances – her own childhood, her perceived limitations – she did the best she knew to do at the time.

When it comes down to it, parents are just people. They have great ideas and not-so-great ideas. They are really smart in some areas and seriously lacking in others. Parents don't become instantly perfect the moment they take on the responsibility of children.

Our total dependence on them as children means that their imperfections affect our entire universe.

That's what makes parenting such an ominous responsibility.

That's why, for *our* children's sake, it is important to reflect and heal…so that we can be the whole, happy, empathic parents that our children need us to be.

However, as sure as we are human, we will make mistakes, too. We will do what we believe is right, but our children will view our actions from *their* perspective. They may believe we were wrong. They may even accuse us of being even hurtful.

My husband and I joke that we should not only have a college education fund for our children, but also a therapy fund. We fully accept that even though we have worked to give them the best childhood imaginable, they may ultimately wish we'd done a thing or two differently.

Our hope is that they accept that we did the best we knew to do, and that they will forgive any mistakes they believe we made.

My husband and I have also modeled the forgiveness we'd like to receive by forgiving our parents of the areas they came up short.

Model forgiveness for your children by forgiving your mom and others who hurt you in the past. Model forgiveness, also, by quickly and easily forgiving your children.

Teaching our children to forgive by being forgiving will increase the chances that our children will forgive us of our imperfections.

The Healing Power of Forgiveness

We forgive others not for their sake, but for our own.

Forgiveness means letting go. Accepting the past instead of arguing with it.

What happened, happened.

And whatever you survived made you a stronger person and a smarter parent.

Holding on to resentment is often an attempt to punish another indefinitely. It is our attempt to ensure that whoever offended us doesn't get away with it.

But if we imprison others with our blame, we remained imprisoned also. We're like a jailer who's keeping an eye on the prisoner…but has to stay in jail, to do so.

Forgiveness frees us to take the life we've been given and make the most of it.

Forgiveness frees us to find the treasure in our past trials. To make our pain productive. To move forward rather than chain ourselves to the past.

Forgiving others also helps us forgive ourselves.

In my view, parents should not even strive to be "perfect." We should strive to do our best, and be open to feedback.

We should be willing to ask forgiveness of our kids, for our inevitable missteps. And we should readily, lovingly forgive ourselves.

We women can be so hard on ourselves sometimes. We act in the moment, then judge our actions for days and years afterward.

I remember a time when my mother was teasing me about the fact that my very articulate 2½ year old daughter wasn't yet potty trained.

As I mentioned, my mother firmly believed that spanking was the best way to teach a child to obey every command – including the command to say, "I've gotta go potty."

Normally, I dismissed my mom's parenting advice. I knew we saw the world differently.

I had been her child. I knew the pain I'd suffered from being beaten to comply with her wishes. I was not about to do that to my child.

Yet, somehow, my mother planted a seed of fear in me during one of her visits. "What if I'm wrong?" I wondered.

"What if Mom is right, and my daughter is pulling one over on me?"

That little seed of fear grew in the back of my mind. And I didn't even realize it, until one day – maybe a week after my mother's visit – when I snapped.

My daughter had gone the entire day making it to the potty. But by 4pm, she was tired, perhaps, and wet her pants.

In a flash, my whole tender-loving-parenting approach few right out the window.

I pulled down her wet training pants and whacked her once on the bottom. "You know how to say 'potty.' I can't believe you did this. Sit here and go potty." I picked her up and placed her on the toilet with just enough force that she knew I was upset.

She sat there, scared, trembling. Then she looked at me standing outside the door. She reached her little arms out to me and said, "Mommy, I love y--," and pulled them back into her lap, hung her head and sobbed.

I saw it right there.

This is how it starts, I thought.

This is where she starts to cut off from me, starts to feel like she can't trust me, starts to hate me. This is how she learns that her body is not hers, she has no rights to it, and she can't protect it from anybody who's bigger than she is.

It was like watching my childhood from the beginning.

I flashed forward 10 years, 20 years, and knew how the rest of the story would go, if I didn't stop it *right then.*

I leaped across the chasm growing between me and my daughter. I put my arms around her and did my best to erase the past 5 minutes.

"I'm sorry, sweetheart. Mommy was wrong. I know you'll go potty when you're ready. Mommy won't hit. I love you."

My daughter was fully potty trained by the age of 4, like most kids. I stepped back, and let her do it in her own time.

When she was about 9 years old, I told her this story. It was still eating me up inside. I still felt guilty. And I wondered if she still suffered from the memory of it.

She didn't remember it at all.

That was one bad day out of thousands of good ones. She had probably forgiven me since the day it happened.

I hadn't forgiven myself.

The more I learned to forgive myself of the mistakes I made as a mother, the more I forgave my mother as well.

I goofed – I still do sometimes. My mom goofed, too.

I may goof less often than Mom did (in my humble opinion), but I'm acting on what *I* know.

My mom acted on what *she* knew.

Letting go of resentment toward my mother allowed me to move forward, and create a new relationship with her, with myself, and with my daughter.

Whether our mothers ask forgiveness or not, whether they admit they were wrong or not, the sooner we forgive and accept our moms as human and fallible – even when we most needed them to be perfect – the sooner we can heal.

Now, let's leave the past and look forward. Let's discuss the principles and tools of the HEART-Based Parenting Approach, and how it can help us raise extraordinary kids.

~ Part II ~

Looking Forward

Becoming the Mom You Wish You'd Had

Chapter 4

Parenting With the End in Mind

I remember feeling panicky as I left the hospital with my first child. I looked around at the doctors and nurses, wondering, "Are they just going to let me take this baby home? I didn't get a degree in this. How does anyone know that I'm qualified to raise this little person?"

When I was 14, McDonald's™ trained me for *9 hours* before leaving me in charge of French fries. Wasn't the job of raising a person so much more important than making French fries?

The hospital staff had taught me how to care for a *baby* – how to nurse and burp her, how to bathe her and swaddle her into a bundle.

But how would I shape this little bundle into a happy, healthy adult? How would I not only care for the baby but raise a *person*?

The job seemed so big and I felt so small. I was terrified.

I never told anyone how scared I was. Not even my husband. Though, I found out years later, he was just as scared that day as I was.

Picturing Your Child 10 Years from Now

As soon as we got home from the hospital, and the baby slept, I began writing and writing in my journal. I wrote about who I hoped my daughter would be as an adult, and what kind of relationship I hoped we would have by then.

Then, just as I'd learned in a Strategic Management course during my Bachelor's program, I began working backwards from the future to the present.

I imagined the kind of qualities I wanted her to have 10-20 years down the road, then worked backwards to figure out, *How do I begin instilling those qualities today?*

I also imagined the kind of relationship I wanted between the two of us 10-20 years down the road, then worked backwards to determine, *How do I begin building that relationship today?*

Parenting can be so stressful that we simply do what works the fastest, with no thought about the long-term consequences.

We let the baby "cry it out" for a few days, so we can have years of quiet nights – but we don't consider how abandoned the baby might feel and how the emotional distance might affect his relationship with us in the teen years.

We smack the 5-year-old in the mouth for saying something we dislike – without thinking we might be teaching her to accept physical abuse in future relationships.

Our children's psyche and self-esteem, as well as their long-term relationship with us, are shaped by these little short-term actions. The more thought we give to our ultimate goal – how we'd like our children to feel about themselves and us – the more we'll make choices that support the result we desire.

As Dr. Phil says: *You're not raising kids, you're raising adults.* The choices you make today should reflect your highest vision for your child tomorrow.

What kind of adults do you want your kids to turn out to be? Do you want them to be self-loving, or self-critical? Would you like them to confidently follow their hearts and make value-based decisions, or to follow the crowd for fear of making a mistake?

In the following exercise you'll explore the question, "What kind of qualities would I like my children to possess 10 years from now?"

It can be easier to see 10 years into the future, than to see 20 years. However, if your child is a newborn, you may want to start at 20 years, then work back to 10.

Exercise 4.1

Close your eyes, and picture the qualities you would like your child to possess 10 years from now. Grab your parenting journal and answer this question:

Ten years from now, when my child is ___ years old, I would like her to have the following qualities:

1.	6.
2.	7.
3.	8.
4.	9.
5.	10.

The list of qualities might include *Responsible, Peaceful, Happy, Committed, Playful, Helpful, Respectful, Loving, Confident, Productive, Thrifty, Strong, Carefree, etc.*

Remember to think about important areas of life – for instance, what qualities would you like her to illustrate when it comes to money? Friends? Recreation? Education?

Now ask:

1. *Am I being these things myself?* Gandhi told us to "Be the change we want to see in the world." You must also "Be" the change you want to see in your family. If you want your kids to be "happy," are you happy? If you want them to be "peaceful," are you peaceful? How can you be the example of the qualities you want for your children?

   Also, if you want your child to be "loving," how can you be more loving toward your child? If you want your child to be "confident" in himself, how can you show you have confidence in him?

2. *How can I help my child to see these qualities in herself?* Acknowledging the smallest example of your child being "helpful" will help her see herself as helpful. Telling your child, "I respect how hard you work at finishing things," rather than, "Ugh, stop being so lazy," will help her see herself as hardworking.

3. *How can I best handle the routine issues of parenthood in a way that supports these qualities?* How can you handle subjects like bedtime, tantrums, potty training, sibling rivalry, mealtimes, and chores, in a way that reinforces the development of great qualities, rather than weakening them?

In the previous chapter, I mentioned the time I listened to my mom instead of my heart, and spanked my daughter because of a potty-training accident.

What helped me get a grip that day, was an image of what I wanted for my daughter 10-20 years down the road.

I wanted my daughter to love herself and to feel at home in her body. I wanted her to feel empowered to protect her personal space.

I realized that, if I wanted her to respect her body as a teenager, and to not let anyone else disrespect it, then I had to show respect for her body, too. Not hit it. Not try to get it to do things (like potty training) that it wasn't ready to do.

I decided I'd rather run the risk that she'd be in diapers until she was 5, than run the risk that I'd short-circuit her respect for her own body.

These were decisions I made based on the soul-searching I did about parenting.

Your soul-searching may lead you to other conclusions. It is not necessary that you interpret everything as I have. The goal is to get you to do some long-range thinking, so that your short-term interactions lead you to the results you intend.

Once you have a clear picture of the end result of your parenting, that picture can guide every decision you make.

Every interaction with our children helps shape the adults they will become. We only have these little people for 18 years or so, but what we do with them can reverberate for the rest of their lives, and the lives of generations to come.

Whether we parent consciously or unconsciously, the fact remains that our actions WILL affect who they become. Our interactions with them today WILL set the tone of our relationship with them tomorrow.

Being mindful about your parenting, acting with thought and intention rather than haphazardly, increases the chances that you'll like the results, that you'll be proud of how you handled the ominous responsibility of parenting.

Picturing Your Relationship 10 Years From Now

This book began with my confession that I didn't like the relationship I'd had with my mom.

More than anything, this is what motivated me to put so much thought into parenting. I was determined to parent differently than she had. I did not want my daughter to one day feel about me the way I felt about my mom.

Do I have any guarantees that my daughter won't resent me or dislike me when she's an adult? No. Although, I think it's hard to resent someone who admits her imperfection, constantly solicits feedback, and encourages freedom of expression.

My primary aim is to create a relationship with her where she feels respected for being who she is, even as I guide her to be her best self.

To me, that's the definition of a great relationship. One where each person feels invited to explore and express who he/she really is.

What do you feel is the most important thing you can give your kid?

From what I've seen, the most important thing a parent can give a kid isn't the latest techno-gadgets. It isn't even the best education money can buy.

More than anything, kids need a great relationship with their parents.

The knowledge that you love them and think the world of them will anchor your children through any of life's potential storms. Good grades or bad, lots of friends or few, your relationship can be a haven, a place where your kid always feels seen, heard, and accepted just for being himself.

Such a relationship is a good model for your child's relationships with others, and with himself.

Think about how your childhood relationship with your mom affected your life. What did you want from her that you never got? I'll bet it's not something she could buy at a store. I'll bet it's something in the relationship. Was it acknowledgement? Respect? Support? Encouragement? Honesty?

How might your life have been different if what was most lacking in that relationship were present in abundance?

As parents we have a unique opportunity to teach our kids how to build healthy relationships by developing a healthy relationship with them.

Our adult children will be better equipped to lovingly talk through differences with their life partners if we teach them how to do it. They will know how to have loving relationships free of blaming, criticizing or manipulating, if our relationship with them is free of these obstacles, too.

Earlier you envisioned the qualities you want your child to possess down the road.

This time, picture the relationship between you and your child? What would you like it to be 10 years from now?

❖ ❖ ❖ ❖ ❖ ❖ ❖ ❖ ❖ ❖ ❖ ❖ ❖ ❖ ❖

Exercise 4.2:

Close your eyes, and picture the relationship you would like to have with your child 10 years from now.

Now grab your parenting journal and answer this question:

Ten years from now, when my child is ___ years old, I would like our relationship to be like this:

1.	6.
2.	7.
3.	8.
4.	9.
5.	10.

Consider these questions:

1. What might your child enjoy most about you?
2. What kinds of things will you do together?
3. How will you reconnect if you seem to be growing distant?
4. What can you do today that will move your relationship one step closer to this vision?

The relationship you want with your child in the future, begins today.

If you want your child's respect, start by respecting her.

If you want your child to listen, listen to her.

If you want her to understand your love and concern for her, show her you understand her point of view.

Below, I've reprinted, with permission, a poem written by Diana Haskins Sterling, author of *Parent as Coach*. Although it was written based on the work she did with teenagers, it beautifully sums up what kids need from parents at any age.

A Message to Parents
If you respect me, I will hear you
If you listen to me, I will feel understood
If you understand me, I will feel appreciated
If you appreciate me, I will know your support
If you support me as I try new things, I will become responsible
And when I am responsible, I will grow to be independent
In my independence, I will grow to love you
and respect you all of my life.
Love, Your Teenager
(Diana Haskins Sterling)

Our ultimate goal as parents is to raise responsible, independent adults, not compliant, obedient children. We want to usher off into the world adults who feel good about themselves and who feel competent to create the lives they want.

We want school-aged kids and teenagers who do what's right even when no one is looking. And adult children with whom we can enjoy positive lifelong relationships.

Our parenting choices today should reflect the outcomes we want tomorrow.

In the next chapter, you will learn more about The 3 Fundamental Beliefs that will support you in creating a mutually loving and respectful relationship with your children.

Chapter 5

The HEART-Based Parenting Approach
~ 3 Fundamental Principles ~

Once, when I was 6, some neighborhood kids stopped by and invited me on a trip to the candy store. My mother was taking a nap, so without even asking, I told them I couldn't go.

"Want us to get you something," they offered.

I made what I thought was a good decision. I chose not to wake my mother, and instead, handed my friends some money I found in the kitchen and placed my order.

I'd forgotten all about it, until my friends came back. My mother, who was awake by then, greeted them and accepted the candy.

She closed the door, then turned to me, "What's this?"

As I began explaining the brilliant thing I had done, her eyes narrowed to little slits and her lips grew tight.

"Who said you could take that money?" she barked at me.

"Nobody…" I lowered my head, knowing I was in trouble.

"You know what it's called when you take something that doesn't belong to you?"

"No," I answered, looking at the floor.

"Stealing."

I quickly looked up. "Stealing" wasn't what I intended to do at all. I thought I was being smart. I thought she'd be proud of me.

"But I thought –"

"Well, you thought wrong. And if you think you're getting this candy, you've got another 'think' coming."

I cried, not because I didn't get the candy, but because I felt completely misunderstood.

What I thought would earn me praise as a good girl who made smart choices, had instead earned me a mean look from Mom and made her see me as a thief.

Belief → Interpretation → Response

There were many incidents like this where my mother's negative beliefs or assumptions about me led her to interpret my intentions as evil. Without investigating, she would react to the evil she perceived.

My mother has often touted her belief that, "Children are manipulative." I would call this her Fundamental Belief about children. The way I see it, this belief was the biggest flaw in her parenting approach.

For, as much as she loved me, she often couldn't hear my attempts to communicate with her because she interpreted them as attempts to control her. She couldn't empathize or be sensitive to my needs, for fear that I would "get the upper hand" or think of myself as "the boss."

Beliefs color our interpretation of another's actions, and therefore dictate our reaction or response.

If Mom's Fundamental Belief had been "Children are Good. They make mistakes based on lack of information," she could have responded more lovingly to mistakes like this one.

Mom could have strengthened our relationship by gently explaining to me what I didn't know. Instead, her hostile reactions pushed me away. Left me feeling alone and misunderstood. Even taught me to be sneaky and hide things I assumed she'd misinterpret.

The point has been made repeatedly throughout this book: What we do with our kids has a lasting effect. Our responses shape their self-image and set the tone of our relationships with them.

Since *beliefs* lead to *interpretations* which determine our *responses* toward our children, **the Fundamental Beliefs we hold about children define the relationships we can have with them.**

Positive beliefs will help us develop a positive relationship. Positive beliefs lead us to interact with our children in a way that helps them feel loved and encouraged to make good decisions and become the best of themselves.

Negative beliefs do exactly the opposite. They create an adversarial relationship, and promote disconnection and mistrust.

HEART-Based vs POWER-Based Parenting

Before we discuss the 3 Fundamental Beliefs which support the HEART-Based Parenting, let's clarify this parenting approach and how it differs from the alternative.

One way parents can define their role in their children's lives is as an enforcer, trainer, or drill sergeant. We can be commanders preparing our troops for battle in the cold, cruel world.

While preparing them for "war," we often wage war with our children. It's Us vs Them. Our will against theirs.

In this parenting approach, our goal is to teach children to obey orders without question.

I call this POWER-Based Parenting. In my mind, POWER stands for Promote Obedience While Encouraging Resentment.

If we rely on the POWER tools in our parenting tool chest – like shaming, yelling, spanking, punishing, manipulating, criticizing – we risk instilling resentment in our children.

We set ourselves up as enemies. We get tangled in power struggles. We believe one of us has to lose for the other one to win.

Using POWER tools with our kids replaces their internal motivation to do what's right with the external motivation to avoid punishment.

Teaching our kids to obey out of fear of punishment robs them of the opportunity to develop an inner sense of discipline. To do good because it feels right to do good.

We interfere with their understanding of themselves and their ability to tune in to an inner voice that can guide them down an authentic path to personal fulfillment.

What I advocate instead is HEART-Based Parenting. HEART, in this case, stands for **Honesty, Empathy, Appreciation, Respect and Time**.

These five principles illustrate the way to build a mutually loving, respectful relationship with children at any age.

Here's a brief description of each principle.

1. **Honesty** – Expressing ourselves lovingly and honestly with our children, and creating an environment where they feel safe being honest with us.

2. **Empathy** – Being able to understand and honor our children's feelings and points of view. Modeling for them how to do the same with us and with others.

3. **Appreciation** – Letting our children know how happy we are to have them in our lives and how their special gifts enrich the family.

4. **Respect** – Treating our children as people, not possessions. Celebrating and promoting their individuality. Giving the respect we wish to receive.

5. **Time** – Showing our kids how important they are to us by spending time having fun with them, and getting to know them. Also, being patient with them as they make mistakes and learn the game of life.

Through HEART-Based Parenting, we not only sustain a lifelong loving relationship with our children, we also help them to become the bright, beautiful, self-motivated young people they came here to be.

We help them become who they are, rather than who we want them to be.

Our children grow up feeling seen, heard, and respected. They maintain love and compassion for themselves and others, because of the love and compassion we show them.

As stated earlier, our beliefs guide our actions.

The HEART-Based parenting approach is based on the following 3 Fundamental Beliefs:

1. The Belief in Your Child's Goodness
2. The Belief in Your Child as an Unfolding Mystery
3. The Belief in Your Child's Need to Learn from Experience

The remainder of this chapter describes, in greater detail, the 3 Fundamental Beliefs of the HEART-Based Parenting Approach.

Belief #1: Belief in Your Child's Goodness

Children pop out of the womb striving to get their needs met. They pucker their mouths looking for food. They cry to bring us closer so we can figure out and satisfy their needs.

The newborn's need to be held close is real and natural. So is his/her need to be fed when hungry.

As children grow, many of their actions continue to be an expression of need. Even behaviors we don't like – tantrums, whining, hitting – are an expression of needs going unmet.

Sometimes it's the need to be heard or the need to establish their own boundaries.

Their needs are good and natural.

Even if the behaviors they use to express the need are socially unacceptable, the need is still real and valid.

If we respond to the need instead of reacting to the (mis)behavior, then we can teach the kid a better way to communicate and satisfy the need.

Believing that children are fundamentally good helps us respond to the needs that prompt their behavior.

Parenting with this level of sensitivity strengthens our relationship with our kids, and supports them in developing a positive self-image.

Belief #2: Belief in Your Child as an Unfolding Mystery

As adults, we often believe we know more than our children know about anything and everything. We even believe we know best about what they should be and do with their lives.

Our kids come through us, but they are not ours.

Our job is not to make them into what we want them to be.

Children possess their own destinies, their own ways of moving through the world. They come here to bring the world a special gift, and we don't necessarily know what it is.

It is revealed over time if we support them in bringing out their individuality instead of trying to shape them into our idea of what they should be.

Seeing children as unfolding mysteries means being open to learning, as they do, who they are, what they're best at, what is most important to them. It means helping them discover and express who they really are.

This belief helps us approach children with the dignity and respect that helps their humanity blossom. It helps us to be receptive to learning from them as much as they learn from us.

Belief #3: Belief in Your Child's Need to Learn from Experience

If life is a school, then the class we take called "Growing Up" is a lab course, not a theory course.

In other words, it's hands on. We must participate, experiment, use trial and error, in order to learn the most about how to be a successful person. It can't all be learned from books or instructions from parents.

Believing children's need to learn from experience helps us to see our children's actions – even the ones we disapprove of – as opportunities for them to learn more about who they are and who they wish to be.

With this firm belief we view mistakes (or misbehavior) not as failures to be punished, but as experiments that facilitate learning.

Mistakes are an important part of learning anything new. Not making mistakes usually means not growing.

The goal of life isn't to avoid all mistakes, it is to learn from them.

With this approach, we help children learn as much as they can from their "experiments." We also understand that they may repeat experiments numerous times to really get the lesson.

These 3 Fundamental Beliefs – the belief in your child's **goodness,** the belief in your child as an **unfolding mystery**, and the belief in your child's need to **learn from experience** – lay a firm foundation on which to develop a healthy relationship with your child.

In my experience, these **3 Fundamental Beliefs** lead adults to interpret children's behavior in the most positive light. Helping us to respond from the HEART, rather than from a place of POWER.

Our loving responses foster a relationship that feels safe for our children to learn to know, love, and express their uniqueness in the world.

The 9 Parenting Tools of the HEART-Based Approach

Each of the 3 Fundamental Beliefs forms a section of parenting toolkit. Each section contains 3 primary tools to help us build strong, effective relationship with our children.

In total, the 9 Parenting Tools of the HEART-Based Parenting Approach are as follows:

Belief in Child's Goodness	1. Empathy
	2. Responsiveness
	3. Closeness
Belief in Child as Unfolding Mystery	4. Self-Knowledge
	5. Self-Expression
	6. Loving Communication
Belief in Child's Need to Learn from Experience	7. Discovery/Exploration
	8. Choices
	9. Guidance

Over the next three chapters, we'll explore the 9 Parenting Tools of the HEART-Based Approach and how they express each of the 3 Fundamental Beliefs.

Chapter 6

The 3 Parenting Tools that Illustrate the Belief in Your Child's Goodness

When my two children were born, and I saw how beautiful, confident, and self-loving they were...my greatest hope was that I wouldn't screw them up.

Have you ever seen a baby with low self-esteem? Have you ever seen one who thinks he doesn't deserve to get what he wants?

Ever seen a newborn girl hide her chubby thighs, or a 3-month-old doubt he was smart enough to roll over?

No. Babies are not born with a low self-image. They don't judge themselves as good or bad. They simply *are*. They exist. And that's enough.

They don't question their worth, intelligence, or goodness. They are fully themselves, unapologetically.

How do kids develop self-esteem issues, then? When do they begin to feel bad about what they do, what they want, and who they are? How do they come to doubt their ability to learn or to be loved?

We teach them.

By ignoring a baby's need to be held, or a toddler's need for self-expression, we teach them to believe they are defective. That they don't deserve to have what they need or want.

When we are unloving, children conclude that they are unlovable. When we treat them badly, they believe they are bad.

On the other hand, when we respect their needs, and behave lovingly toward them, they feel loved. They believe they are lovable. We treat them well and they believe they are good.

Children don't judge themselves as good or bad until we project those judgments onto them, through our loving or hostile interactions with him.

Firmly believing in our children's goodness helps us to uncover the need behind their behavior, and to acknowledge and respect those needs.

This belief is "hammered out" with the following 3 Parenting Tools: **Empathy, Responsiveness,** and **Closeness.** Let's look at each of these separately.

HEART-Based Parenting Approach Toolkit – Tool 1: Empathy

The cornerstone of any good relationship is Empathy.

Empathy is the ability to honor another's feelings without judgment. To respect their pain, or their joy. to understand their point of view, even if it differs from yours.

When we firmly believe our children are good, we are less likely to interpret their mistakes as malicious.

If the kid does something we disagree with, we look underneath the behavior to see what's motivating it. We help them find a healthier way of meeting that need.

For instance, when my son, Buddy, was just a year old, he was gaga about his 3-year-old sister who enjoyed entertaining him. Every time she did something funny, he would reach out and hit her or bite her.

I watched his little face, and noticed the way his eyes lit up right before he struck. And his glowing smile afterward.

Believing this boy to be nothing but good, I could see that this act that looked a lot like violence had absolutely no malice behind it.

It was a genuine act of love. A crime of passion, if you will.

My son's love for his sister was so huge, that all he wanted to do was make contact with her. For whatever reason, it came out as a bite or a hit.

Instead of punishing or yelling at him, I verbalized the feeling behind the act. "You've got big love for Jasi, don't you?" Then I showed him a better way to express his love. "Don't hit...hug," (as I hugged Jasi, who was starting to cry). Or "We only bite food...but you can *kiss* Jasi, like this..."

Within a year, Buddy learned to show his enormous love for his sister in positive ways.

Had I reacted to and punished his behavior without understanding what was driving it, the end result might have been different. I might have spoiled those great feelings he had for her, or simply taught him to believe that he was bad.

Who knows?

Parents who believe that children are bad and must be taught to be good, tend to have a minimal sense of empathy. They can't see life from the child's perspective. They can't respond from a place of sensitivity.

Instead, they stick with their own perspective, focus on how the kids' behavior embarrasses or inconveniences them as adults, and react from a place of self-interest.

Parents who have little or no sense of empathy see only the "wrong" in their children's inconvenient behaviors. Everything from crying babies to fighting siblings is an evil to be trained or beaten out of them.

This leaves the child's needs unacknowledged and unmet.

Some kids resort to more offensive behavior in a more desperate attempt to be heard. Other kids drive their feelings underground and resign themselves to being misunderstood.

On the other hand, when we firmly believe that children are fundamentally good – that they are good little people with good hearts and good intentions – we can accept their feelings without judging them.

We can respond to their needs without questioning their motives.

When we accept their feelings and their point of view, we can act out of love, and not out of fear of being manipulated, or fear of losing the "battle of wills."

Empathy helps us feel and act tenderly toward our children, even when we feel annoyed by their behavior.

Parenting with empathy, we support our children's right to feel what they feel and think what they think – even if it's inconvenient for us.

This doesn't mean that we give in to every whim. Nor that we satisfy every need immediately...just that we acknowledge the need, continue to see the child as good, and approach him/her with gentleness and sensitivity.

Empathy is the most important tool in the HEART-Based Parenting toolkit. Everything else stems from it.

Following are a few ideas on how to tap the power of empathy with children at any age.

❖ ❖ ❖ ❖ ❖ ❖ ❖ ❖ ❖ ❖ ❖ ❖ ❖ ❖ ❖
Exercise 6.1: Tapping the Power of Empathy

Newborns
Imagine you were abruptly transported to an alien planet, run by giants who speak a language you don't understand.

Your arms and legs don't work in this atmosphere, so you are totally dependent on these giants to meet everyone of your needs – including the need to feel safe and to relieve any discomfort. And you haven't a clue how to get them to understand you.

Let such a fantasy connect you deeply with your baby's cries. Step into those tiny shoes and sense what it feels like to be small and helpless.

Toddlers
1. **Talk About Feelings.** As toddlers develop language skills, frequently use words like *Angry, Sad, Happy, Scared, Lonely, Excited* to help them learn that feelings have names.

This will help both you and your child to practice tuning into what the child is feeling.

2. **Check In.** Ask toddlers regularly, "How are you feeling?" If they can't answer, make your best assumption and speak it out loud, "You sure look happy right now."

   This will show your children that you care about their feelings, while teaching them to be self aware and to use language to express themselves.

3. **Verbalize.** Next time your child is upset or throwing a tantrum, ask, "How are you feeling," or make a good guess & verbalize it ("You seem really angry right now. Is that right?")

   Don't react to the feeling, just respect it. And empathize with it. Remember, his feelings are about him, not about you.

4. **Accept Feelings and Desires.** Never deny or belittle your child's feelings. Accept his right to feel whatever he feels, and want whatever he wants (whether he can have it or not, he has a right to want it).

School-Aged / Teens

1. **See His/Her Point of View.** Practice hearing and sensing your child's point of view whenever she is speaking.

2. **Empathize.** Listen for clues that tell you what it's like to be her – rather than for clues that she needs your advice or leadership.

3. **Ask.** Make a practice of asking, "What was that like for you?" And "What did you want most in that situation?"

This will show her you honestly care about her experience. It will also help you learn more about her and understand what's important to her.

When we parent with empathy, we are responsive, instead of reactive....which leads us to Parenting Tool #2.

HEART-Based Parenting Approach Toolkit – Tool 2: Responsiveness

The most natural result of empathy is Responsiveness.

When you can feel the need behind your child's behavior, then you can respond to the need and not react to the behavior.

It may be a great gift, that babies can't talk for the first 1-2 years. Their cryptic cries require us to try different ways to soothe them in our attempt to understand the need they're communicating.

This gives us practice interpreting and responding to their needs instead of reacting to their behaviors.

The skill of interpreting and responding to the need behind the behavior is just as important once kids can talk. And it can feel just as challenging.

Since the age of 12, my daughter has developed the capacity to be moody. She is generally a cheerful, engaging girl. But without warning, she can flash a nasty attitude and flurry of verbal hostility.

It is tempting to send her to her room, or somehow make distance from her when she's being irritable.

Who wants to be around that, right?

However, when I challenge myself to tend to the need behind her behavior, I always find that what she needs is MORE closeness when she's in a funky mood, not less.

When I pull her closer by looking in her eyes, and speaking softly to her, the mood subsides more quickly.

When we spend more time together, talking and having fun, the moody spells happen less frequently.

Responding lovingly to our children's needs affirms that they are good and their needs are important to us. They learn that, even when their tactics are annoying, we know that at their core, they are good.

When we react to a kid's surface behavior, we miss the opportunity to address the need below the surface. We miss a chance to bond with them and show the strength of our love.

We risk alienating them, leaving their needs unmet, and having them resort to less healthy behaviors in her attempt to be heard.

Remember, responding to needs doesn't mean satisfying every want.

A child who *wants* candy for breakfast, still *needs* good nutrition instead. As parents, we can empathize with the child's desire for candy – what adult hasn't eaten a donut for breakfast, at least once? But we can respond to the *need* for nourishment by supplying real food.

(A highly aware parent might even overhear that an intense craving for sweets can indicate a vitamin deficiency, and therefore, add more veggies and fruit to the kid's diet – again, responding to the *need* behind the behavior.)

Parenting responsively calls us to be insightful and inquisitive. It keeps us open to information coming from our children, our instincts, and the environment.

Most of all, parenting responsively is an expression of the belief in our child's goodness.

Responsiveness communicates unconditional love. It strengthens our children's trust that we understand and accept them for who they really are, even when they can't express themselves the way they want.

Exercise 6.2: Practicing Responsiveness vs Reactivity

Here are a few ways to ensure you're responding to children's needs rather than reacting to their behavior.

Newborns

1. **Look and listen** – for the need behind each cry. Close your eyes and hold the baby during crying spells. Sense with your intuition or spirit what the baby is trying to tell you.
2. **Keep Close.** Consider how keeping the baby close will help him/her feel more secure and welcomed on this "alien planet."
3. **First, Do No Harm.** Be mindful of how harshness or rejection may instill feelings of fear, unlovable-ness, and emotional distance in the baby that you'll continue to deal with in the teen years.

Toddlers

1. **Respect** the toddler's need for independence, exploration, and self-definition. Hear those needs in every "No." Feel them in every tantrum.
2. **Celebrate.** Instead of labeling a toddlers' new self-expression skills as "defiance," see the good in them. Celebrate the start of their journey to figure out who they are and who they want to be.
3. **Empathize** with a toddler's need or desire even if it cannot be satisfied in the moment. Say something like, "I understand that you want the book, sweetheart. And it's frustrating not to get what you want. But we're not getting it

right now. How about we stop at the library tonight and you choose what you want?"

School-Aged / Teens

1. **Feel the Need.** Just as with newborns and toddlers, do your best to see and ask about the need behind your teen's behaviors.
2. **Be Curious.** Ask them with sincerity and curiosity (not judgment or sarcasm) "What are you hoping to gain from this? What do you really want? How is this serving you?"
3. **Brainstorm.** Help teens brainstorm new ideas and approaches that may better satisfy their needs.

❖ ❖ ❖ ❖ ❖ ❖ ❖ ❖ ❖ ❖ ❖ ❖ ❖ ❖ ❖

A sensitive approach to parenting draws our kids closer, rather than pushing them away from us.

If we want our kids to feel close to us in later years, it behooves us to cultivate that closeness right now. Today.

This takes us to Parenting Tool #3: Closeness.

HEART-Based Parenting Approach Toolkit – Tool 3: Closeness

Many parents worry that keeping their children close (physically and emotionally) will make them needy and clingy.

They fear that kids will never become self-confident individuals if kept close, so they prematurely attempt to wean kids of their dependency.

They rush to instill "*self*-sufficiency." They let babies "cry it out" so they'll learn to *self*-soothe. They ignore toddlers' cries for help, so they'll become *self*-reliant.

Then, when the kid is older and emotionally distant, parents ask, "Why won't you talk to me?" Or when the kid gets into trouble trying to manage a big problem on his own, parents ask, "Why didn't you come to me?"

My husband and I discovered that Abraham Maslow was right. In his "Hierarchy of Needs," Maslow explained that satisfying lower level needs (like safety and security) naturally leads a person to progress on to higher level needs (like self-confidence and self-esteem).

When our kids were 7 and 5, they announced (to our delight) that they were ready to leave the Family Bed and sleep in their own beds.

When they were babies, we decided it was unfair for the littlest people in the house to have to sleep alone while the biggest people got to share each other's company. So we practiced the Family Bed.

(Right here is where people often ask, "How did you...you know...have sex?" The answer is: We had sex everywhere in the house <u>except</u> our bed. I apologize if that's too much information, but you were bound to ask, sooner or later.)

The point is, we kept our kids as close as they needed to be for as long as they needed it.

When their need for nighttime closeness was satisfied, when they felt safe and secure, they moved on.

In an earlier chapter, we described the relationships we'd like to have with our kids when they're older.

If we want a close relationship with them then, why not foster that closeness now?

What sense does it make to push kids away when they're little and then try to draw them in when they're older?

Even as teenagers, our kids still need to feel close to us. Many of the problems we experience with teens come from our insistence on pushing them too far away from us too soon.

My friends who have made it a point to maintain a genuine, close relationship with their kids, don't seem to have the typical relationship meltdowns with their teens that most parents believe are unavoidable.

When teens feel close to their parents – when they feel seen, heard, understood, and appreciated – there is no need to rebel.

Here are a few ways to develop and maintain a close, loving relationship with kids of any age.

❖ ❖ ❖ ❖ ❖ ❖ ❖ ❖ ❖ ❖ ❖ ❖ ❖ ❖ ❖

Exercise 6.3: Maintaining Closeness with Kids

<u>Newborns</u>

1. **Together Time.** Spend as much time with your newborn as you can. If your personality and living situation can support it, stay-at-home parenting, can be a worthwhile investment in your long-term relationship with your child.

2. **Physical Touch.** Babies thrive on physical touch. So, be in physical contact with your baby as much as possible. Again, if your personality and living situation are amenable, co-sleeping, nursing, and carrying the baby on your body can be great ways to keep a baby close and secure.

3. **Get Creative.** If none of the above is feasible for you, get creative. Invest as much "together time" as you possibly can. Do your best to plant the seed that "Time with mommy is great." You'll reap the benefits in later years.

Toddlers

1. **Play.** Play, play, play with your toddler. Play is where toddlers do their greatest learning. Bring out your inner child and play with toys. Dance around the house together. Make up silly songs. Make FUN your first priority.

2. **Read.** Sharing stories together strengthens your bond. Stories give you and your child a common language, a set of metaphors to use when talking about life. As in, "Are you angry like the fish in *Cat in the Hat*?" Or, "You were brave, like *Sheila Rae*."

3. **Watch TV** **Together.** Like books, kids' TV shows also provide you and your toddler with a common language. So, if your toddlers watch TV at all (not necessary, but many do), try to spend at least half the time watching *with* them, instead of using it to occupy them while you get other things done. In this way, TV can bring you closer rather than keeping you apart.

School-Aged/Teens

1. **Stay Close.** Remember that even though they have their own friends and separate lives, older kids still need to feel close to you.

   Keep at least one night per week as Family Time (even more is better). Take turns choosing how to spend this time. Cooking, hiking, videos, board games are some great choices.

Spending more time talking together, than quietly watching something, is best.

2. **1-on-1.** At least once a month, spend 1-on-1 time with each kid.

Having fun together on a regular basis strengthens your relationship and reminds children how important they are to you.

Staying close to your children, physically and emotionally, is another way to illustrate your belief in their goodness. Closeness keeps you tuned into their needs and keeps them secure in their connection to you.

Empathy + Responsiveness + Closeness

Kids pop out of the womb whole, perfect, and beautiful. They love themselves completely. They have no shame and reject no part of themselves.

They don't judge themselves as good or bad. They just "are."

They don't judge their needs as right or wrong. They simply do whatever it takes to their needs fulfilled.

If their needs are fulfilled, they develop a positive self-image. They see themselves as worthy and lovable.

If their needs are not fulfilled, they tend to develop a lower self-image. They feel unworthy, and unlovable.

Seeing children as fundamentally good means interacting with them expressing Empathy + Responsiveness + Closeness.

These qualities help us stay open to our children as they develop into the unique individuals they came here to be.

When we empathize with and respond to their needs, and stay physically and emotionally close to them, our children trust that we know and love them, and they develop the confidence that they can get what they need in life.

I think of this type of parenting, HEART-Based Parenting, as providing a Magic Mirror for your child.

If you're old enough, you may remember the TV show Romper Room. The host would look into her Magic Mirror and "see" the kids in the viewing audience. "I see Mary, and Sally, and Johnny and Steve..."

Kids watching (with those names) felt SEEN. (Tough luck for kids like me, with non-traditional names...but I never stopped hoping.)

Similarly, our children want to be SEEN by us. They feel most secure when they know we really see *them* – not just their flaws, not just our ideas of what they should or could be, but who they really *are*.

The 3 Parenting Tools described in the next chapter are based on the second fundamental belief of the HEART-Based Parenting Approach: The belief that each child is an **Unfolding Mystery**.

Believing in the inherent goodness of children, and honoring the mystery of who they are becoming, make us an affirming presence in our children's lives – helping them become their best selves.

Chapter 7

The 3 Parenting Tools that Illustrate the Belief in Your Child as an Unfolding Mystery

Imagine someone placed a seed in your hand and left you responsible for bringing it to its fullest potential. There's no picture or note indicating what kind of tree or plant it is to become. You are simply required to care for it as best you can and discover, as the seed slowly reveals, what it is meant to be.

A child is like that seed.

Each child comes here with his/her own unique path. Our job, as parents, is not to define the path, but to help discover it.

When my daughter was a toddler, I did everything I could to shape her into a rough-and-tumble tomboy instead of a soft-and-prissy girl. I avoided pink clothes like the plague. Bought her as many toy trucks as dolls. Dressed her in overalls and hiking boots – never, ever a dress.

Having felt so vulnerable and victimized as a little girl, I intended to raise a fighter, not a princess.

Funniest thing happened when my daughter was 3 years old. My mother bought her a dress. My daughter tried it on, and wouldn't take it off. She insisted on sleeping in it.

The next morning, I knew from the way she gazed into the mirror, smoothing the dress with her hands, that I had, not the tomboy I wanted, but a certifiable "girly-girl." *Where did that come from*, I wondered. I certainly hadn't encouraged it.

I quickly came to accept that, when it came to personal expression, my daughter had her own agenda. She already had, inside of her, a blueprint of who she was.

Trying to remake her into an image I held would be a waste of time, and a violation of her individuality. So, instead, I committed to learning who she was meant to be and how I could be support her in being that.

When kids are free to express themselves, they easily tell us everything we need to know about who they are and who they're meant to be.

Ever hear of kids who never stop drumming at the kitchen table? Kids who can't sit still and focus on anything but building with blocks? Kids who make fast friends and can't stop talking in class?

Kids' likes and dislikes, their styles of relating to people and things, the behaviors they seem most attached to – all give us clues about who they are meant to be.

When we set aside our own agendas and pay attention to our children's clues, we support them in living authentic, passionate lives. We spotlight and affirm their existing strengths instead of trying to replace them with different ones.

Parents who ignore their children's uniqueness and, instead, try to shape them to fit a certain mold, risk cutting children off from themselves, and from the parents.

They risk developing a relationship where kids don't feel seen, heard, or respected for who they are. Or worse, a relationship where the kids completely lose touch with who they are and disconnect from their own creativity.

Our responsibility as parents is to help our children grow to be what they came here to be - to provide the *space* for them to explore their uniqueness and the *tools* to develop their natural gifts.

Fostering our children's "unfolding" involves staying open to their signs, strengths, and style.

It means letting go of the notion that we know all there is to know about them.

It means letting go of the desire to chisel them into our image, or any other image, and instead, inviting them to know, love, and express themselves authentically.

The 3 Parenting Tools that encourage our children's mysteries to unfold, are valuing **Self-Knowledge, Self-Expression,** and **Loving Communication.**

These are numbers 4, 5, and 6 of the 9 Parenting Tools of the HEART-Based Parenting Approach. Let's explore each.

HEART-Based Parenting Approach Toolkit – Tool 4: Self-Knowledge

From an early age, adults applaud kids for learning everything there is to know *outside* of themselves. We're delighted when they count to 10, recite the alphabet, name the planets.

So much of kids' energy is spent learning "facts" that, many young people enter adulthood knowing a lot about many things in the world, but nearly nothing about themselves.

I was one of those young people.

From the time I learned to read at age 3, until the day I earned my Bachelor's degree, "performing well" academically was my top priority. By the time I graduated college, I knew things about marketing and calculus and literature, but I didn't know the first thing about myself.

I couldn't say what I thought about politics or history. I didn't know what my strengths were (beyond taking exams) or what I really wanted to do with my life.

I spent 4 years getting a bachelor's degree in marketing, only to find out, a month into my first real job, that working in "Corporate America" would bore me out of my mind.

How did I manage to get so far down a path that wasn't right for me? How did I interview for jobs, saying things like, "I'm a team player," when, actually, I work best solo?

I had a grasp of a few facts and statistics, but I was completely out of touch with myself.

Kids these days may be at even greater risk for growing out of touch with themselves.

With an increased emphasis on standardized test scores, and schools so competitive that even kindergartens can require interviews and essays, there is more pressure for kids to "learn facts" and "perform well" than ever before.

Yet, to paraphrase a common Bible scripture, *What does it profit a kid to gain the whole world and lose his own soul?*

Each child comes to this world with a unique path. Their preferences, strengths, and values are the clues they must follow to discover that path.

To live an authentic life – a life that fits them just right – it is just as important for kids to learn about themselves as it is for them to learn about the world around them.

Factual knowledge without self-knowledge can lead to abundance on the outside, but leave us feeling empty on the inside.

We may feel like the life we're living isn't really ours. We risk the fate that motivational speaker Wayne Dyer calls, "Dying with our music still inside us."

Self-knowledge doesn't just pay off when choosing careers and life partners in the adult years.

Knowing, loving, and respecting themselves, helps teens fight peer pressure.

When they know and love who they are, they make choices that take them where they want to go instead of those that lead them off track.

Self-aware children are better equipped to make choices that reflect who they really are and who they most want to be.

Understanding who they are and what they value helps even the youngest children make the self-directed choice to do what's right even when no adult is around.

I have observed this in my own children.

My 14 year old daughter is amazing, the way she enjoys having friends but has no desire to "follow the crowd." The way she measures her peers using herself as the standard, instead of the other way around.

She is comfortable in her own skin, with friends or alone. She knows what she likes, and couldn't care less about others' approval.

My son, since he could talk, has been the kid other moms trust to keep their kids in line.

He trusts his instincts about everything from people to websites. And "listens" to his body to eat healthy and avoid junk food and allergy triggers.

He's diligent and self-managing with his chores. And is eagerly helpful around the house.

Parenting them, I've learned that self-knowledge promotes self-discipline.

The sooner we can promote self-discipline in our children, by helping them to connect with their inner reasons for good behavior, the less we'll need to rely on external motivators.

We can help our kids tune into themselves by making self-knowledge a priority. Like a mirror, we can help our kids reflect on their lives. Help them to see and to know themselves intimately.

Making self-knowledge a priority means it is just as important that our kids know what they want as it is that they know what we want.

It means that getting them to think about the natural consequences of their actions is equally or more important than us inventing consequences for their actions.

Here are just a few age-appropriate ideas for promoting a child's self-knowledge.

❖ ❖ ❖ ❖ ❖ ❖ ❖ ❖ ❖ ❖ ❖ ❖ ❖ ❖ ❖

Exercise 7.1: Promoting Your Child's Knowledge of Self

Here are just a few age-appropriate ways to help strengthen your child's connection to his/her inner self:

Newborns / Toddlers

1. **Be a Mirror.** Mirror to your children all the beauty and goodness that they are. Talk to them about their bodies and feelings in glowing terms.

   Even what fills a diaper should be spoken about positively, because it's a part of the child. "Did you make mama a present? Wow, what a big present from such a big boy!"

2. **Accentuate the Positive.** Speak positively about your kids – to them and to others – so they learn how awesome, lovable, and worthy they are.

School-Aged

1. **Get to Know Them.** Ask your kids regularly about what they like and dislike. Help them go deeper by asking, "What

do you like/dislike about it? What would make it better? How would you change it?"

2. **Value Their Perspective.** Show that you're interested in how they think and feel about things. Value their opinion and perspective.

The more they understand that you really want to know them, the more inspired they'll be to deeply know themselves.

Teens

1. **Ask About Differing Perspectives.** As teens develop into complex individuals, they have mixed feelings about situations and people in their lives. They are also able to hold their own and another's perspective simultaneously.

   Ask, "What are some of the other feelings you have about this?" And, "How do you imagine this looks from your friend's point of view?"

2. **Explore His/Her Point of View.** Get into the habit of asking questions that keep your teen exploring her own point of view, values, expectations, and interpretations.

   Remember, the goal is to support her in knowing who she is, what she thinks and believes, what makes her tick academically, professionally, and socially.

   A few good starter questions are:

   a. What was that like for you?
   b. How'd you feel when that was happening?
   c. On a scale of 1-10, how important is this to you?

A few pointers:

1. Ask open-ended questions – not questions that can be answered with "Yes" or "No." Start questions with words like "What" and "How," to spark deeper, more thoughtful answers.

2. Avoid asking, "Why?" Why-questions tend to provoke defensiveness and justification instead of introspection and self-knowledge.

3. Don't interrogate. Only ask a few questions, not a list of them.

4. Accept that your kid may not answer right away. You may not get an answer at all. The questions are more for them than for you.

5. Don't judge. Your child's answers will reflect her evolving sense of self. They may shift as she grows. Leave her time and space to figure out who she is. Your questions will help her think out loud, so she can hear and evaluate who she is becoming.

Fostering self-knowledge, or self-awareness, helps kids stay connected to themselves, and rooted in their values.

The next Parenting Tool – Valuing Self-Expression – is the logical next step. For Self-Expression empowers them to bring out the self they find within – to live and love what is true for them.

HEART-Based Parenting Approach Toolkit – Tool 5: Self-Expression

Were you allowed to express your full range of emotions as a kid? Were you as encouraged to say, "I'm angry," or "I don't like this," as you were to say, "I'm so excited," or "I love you?"

Was there space in your family to voice your feelings, thoughts, opinions, even if they differed from others?

It may have been unintentional, but my mom made it clear, when I was a kid, that my not-so-happy feelings were not as welcomed as my happier ones.

If I expressed anger in typical kid fashion – crying, hitting, tantrums – my mother wouldn't help me express my feelings more constructively, instead she punished the behavior so severely that it felt like the emotion behind it was being punished as well.

As a result, I grew out of touch with my feelings – especially my anger.

As an adult, this led to problems in my marriage. I didn't know how to talk about things that upset me, so I stuffed my anger down deep and let small issues grow into big ones. Eventually a wall of pain built up between me and my husband that took us years to resolve.

Even as I struggled to express my own anger, I was determined not to let my daughter learn the same bad habits.

I became aware of my daughter's anger when she was 3 ½. She had always been adorably blissful (after the teething stages anyway), so I was confused when she became moody and uncooperative.

At the time I didn't connect it to the birth of her brother (they're 2 ½ years apart), because she didn't direct her anger at her brother. She directed it at me. And I wasn't sure what I was doing to provoke it.

Not knowing how to deal with my own anger, I was clueless about how to deal with my daughter's. *How can I accept her anger without condoning her lashing out? How can I teach her to honor all of her feelings when anger and conflict scare me so much?*

One day, during a family road trip, my husband and I noticed her singing along with an Alanis Morissette cd. She couldn't make out the words (fortunately, because some are profane), but with her nonsensical substitutes she matched the intense feeling in the angry songs.

That's when I got an idea for how to help her work out her angry feelings.

When we returned home, I stuck a microphone in her hand, connected it to the stereo, stood her on the coffee table, and let her sing along with songs like, "You Oughtta Know."

I didn't know what to do with her anger, but I didn't want to drive it underground. I hoped the angry songs would at least keep her connected to her feelings until she could find the language to express them constructively.

Soon, she was able to tell me that she didn't like how, at bedtime, I always "cuddled" with her little brother first – nursing him to sleep – and then cuddled with her second.

It was the sweetest, most honest expression of, "I don't like coming second all the time," that I had ever heard.

Had I not helped her feel safe enough to express herself, I would never have known that what made perfect sense to me – nursing the younger kid before cuddling with the older – left her feeling like a second class citizen.

That's how we started "Taking Turns," alternating every night which kid got "First Cuddle."

And that's how Jasmine learned to say, "Mommy, I need to talk to you," when she was upset about something.

Whether it's emotions, or hair style, or creative talent, kids must be allowed to express themselves if they are ever to discover who they are.

Self-expression is the active part of self-knowledge. When fostering self-knowledge, we encourage kids to look within, and find the truth of themselves.

To foster self-expression, we must create a safe space for children to bring the true "self" out into the world.

The family that accepts the whole person – that doesn't applaud the expression of certain parts of the self, while "boo-ing" the expression of other parts – is a family that feels loving and safe for each family member to "unfold" into the fullness of him- or herself.

Exercise 7.2: Encouraging Self-Expression

Newborns

1. **Encourage Self-Expression.** Drop the phrase, "Don't cry," from your vocabulary. Start now to develop the habit of encouraging self-expression. Instead try, "Yes, yes" or "I hear you sweetie…" while comforting the baby.

2. **Be Responsive.** Respond to newborns as immediately as possible. Feed them when they're hungry, not on a schedule

that's convenient for you. Hold them or talk to them when they're upset.

Babies don't understand "delayed gratification." They live in the now. Either something good is happening now, or it isn't happening.

Efforts to teach a newborn to be patient – like delaying or scheduling feedings – may do more harm than good, if they also teach that the world is an unresponsive place.

Toddlers / School-Aged

1. **Pay Attention** to the behaviors, even the irksome ones, that your kid seems most attached to – e.g., drumming, humming, climbing, jumping, dumping toys out on the floor.

   Be open to understanding the importance of these behaviors to your kid. Instead of discouraging them, find creative ways to allow them, maybe in a contained space, as the kid explores, and expresses, who he/she is.

2. **Practice Being Present** when emotions run high. Don't rush to thoughts about how you wish you or your kid were feeling. Accept what is being felt now, and trust that by allowing its expression, feelings eventually change.

   Use the language of "I feel…" rather than, "You make me feel…" Teach yourself and your kids to own and verbalize feelings without blaming, criticizing, or trying to change the other person.

Teens

1. **Respect Feelings and Thoughts.** Respect the teen's right to every feeling and thought.

If you object to how your teen chooses to *express* feelings and thoughts, first, restate the feeling or thought – let him/her know you're listening and really hearing what's being said.

Then, honestly share your feelings about how the teen expressed himself. NOT in an effort to change her, but to let her know how you were affected. And work together to come up with ways of self-expression that feel good to both of you.

As in, "I'm glad you shared with me how angry you are. And I totally understand why. But when you were yelling, I felt tense. I kinda closed up. And it was harder for me to hear you. Can we come up with a way for you to let me know how angry you are without yelling, so I can hear you a little easier next time?"

2. **Respect Their Point of View.** Let teens know that you respect their point of view. Teens, like everyone, like to be with people who "get" them.

   Ask, "What's your opinion on this?" Ask for their feedback and input into family decisions.

When we let children know that we love and accept all of them – not just the parts that please us – we make our homes into places where kids feel respected, seen, and heard.

By inviting them to explore and express their individuality, we give them the practice they'll need to be fully themselves as adults – on the job, in their marriages, and wherever life takes them.

The *way* we express ourselves is as important as the *fact* that we express ourselves.

With the next Parenting Tool – Loving Communication – we model healthy communication skills for our kids, as we use words that build up instead of tearing down.

HEART-Based Parenting Approach Toolkit – Tool 6: Loving Communication

Chapter 2 highlighted the importance of acknowledging the things our mothers got right, and of learning as much from her successes as from her mistakes.

I am happy to acknowledge that "Loving Communication" is one of my mother's greatest strengths.

A devout, Bible-quoting Christian, she lives according to the scripture, "The power of life and death is in the tongue." She tries always to use her words to promote life.

My mom learned how hurtful words could be from the mistakes her mom and family had made. So she is careful with her words when she speaks to me and my siblings.

For example, when she was small, my mom experienced some temporary periodontal issues, and family members teased her about her teeth.

For years after the problem was resolved, she still covered her mouth when she laughed.

As a result of that experience, my mom makes sure to never use words that made her kids feel ugly.

My mom's mother also repeatedly told her children that she'd never wanted kids, and that kids cramped her style. Due to that painful experience, my mother makes it a point to always tell us how much we are loved and wanted.

Her words of support and affirmation have helped me and my 3 siblings to feel loved and appreciated in spite of any mistakes she's made.

If words from anyone contain "the power of life and death" with children, then words from parents, specifically, contain that power magnified by 1000. Parents' words can comfort or sting greater than anyone else's.

Our words tell our kids how we see them, and shape how they see themselves. If, in our words, they hear that they are lovable and fantastic, they will learn to see themselves as lovable and fantastic.

If, on the other hand, they hear us judging and criticizing, then they'll learn to judge and criticize themselves.

The truth is, our children *are* lovable and fantastic, each in his own way. Their mission is to discover their "own way" of being all the wondrous things they are.

Our words can either be stepping stones or obstacles on our kids' road to discovering their own magic.

The messages we send, through our words, as well as our actions, go straight into the hearts of our children. There is virtually no filter, no protective shield to slow down the arrows we sling at them.

Warm messages go right to work building our kids up; critical messages immediately begin tearing them down.

To help our children stay connected to the wonder of themselves, to help them to discover their mysterious potential and unfold into the best of themselves, we must be mindful of the messages we send.

❖ ❖ ❖ ❖ ❖ ❖ ❖ ❖ ❖ ❖ ❖ ❖ ❖ ❖ ❖

Exercise 7.3: Communicating HEART-to-HEART

Since our messages go straight into the hearts of our kids, HEART is a great acronym to describe a way to ensure we communicate our love and support for our kids.

Here's how the HEART-Based parenting model applies directly to communication:

1. **Honesty** – Instead of judging or criticizing your child's behavior, share your concerns, honestly, as what they really are: Your thoughts and feelings.

   Instead of saying, "You're lazy. You'll never make it to college this way," let her know, "I feel worried about your future. I think it may be hard for you to get accepted into college with these grades."

   Also, make your relationship safe for your kids to be honest with you. Addressing and re-directing unwanted behavior, instead of punishing it, will keep the lines of communication open. Do your best to give them no reason to lie or hide things from you.

2. **Empathy** – We explored earlier the role of empathy in building a strong relationship with children. Striving to understand your child's perspective delivers the message that you honor him as an individual and care deeply about his feelings and desires.

    Show him you care as much about his perspective as your own, by sharing more questions than answers. Ask, "You sound angry. Is that right?" And then, "Tell me more about what has you so upset."

    Then be big enough to empathize, apologize, admit you're wrong if that's the case. "I feel sad that what I did left you feeling hurt. What would you like me to do differently next time?"

3. **Appreciation** – Remind your kids how valuable and important they are by telling them how much you appreciate them and what they do.

    Talk about the good things kids do more often than the "bad" things.

    Say "I appreciate your for doing…" or "I appreciate the way you did…"

4. **Respect** – If you want kids to respect you, start by respecting them. Respect is a two-way street. Set the example that you want them to follow.

    Show your respect by listening when they talk, assuming the best instead of the worst, supporting their individuality.

    Speak your respect, as Diana Sterling suggests in her book, *Parent as Coach*. Instead of praising their actions, as in, "I'm so proud of your for getting good grades," acknowledge the person behind the action, as in, "I respect your courage / commitment / thoroughness / dedication to completing the job / loyalty to your friends."

5. **Time** – Time is another powerful way to communicate love to your child. What we love and enjoy most, we spend the most time with. The time you spend with your kids lets them know how important they are to you.

Remember, childhood only lasts for a short time. Drink it in. Savor it. When it's gone, it's gone.

❖ ❖ ❖ ❖ ❖ ❖ ❖ ❖ ❖ ❖ ❖ ❖ ❖ ❖ ❖

When we are mindful to communicate lovingly with our children, we remain open to them as they change and grow. We support them as they figure out who they are and who they want to be.

Loving Communication means communicating with empathy. Understanding the long-range power of our words and actions. Being mindful to build them up instead of tearing them down – promoting the best in them instead of trying to stamp out the worst in them.

Judgment, labels, and harshness close us off from our kids. Kids don't feel safe "unfolding" – discovering and defining themselves – in relationships that are hurtful.

By communicating our love tenderly, we make the relationship safe for our kids to "unfold" *within* it, instead having to define themselves *outside* of it.

Self-Knowledge + Self-Expression + Loving Communication

Helping our kids connect to their unlimited potential is perhaps our most important task as parents.

Supporting our kids in **knowing** who they are and **expressing** their uniqueness in the world, as well as **lovingly communicating** our support of their individuality, helps our children to become the best young people they can be.

Coming up next, in the last chapter, we'll explore The 3 Parenting Tools that illustrate the Belief in Your Child's Need to Learn from Experience.

Chapter 8

The 3 Parenting Tools that Illustrate the Belief in Your Child's Need to Learn from Experience

Life is a hands-on game. The only way to learn the game of life is to jump in and play.

We can't learn any game or sport just by having experts tell us how it's done. We have to get our hands dirty, experience it, learn what works and what doesn't.

And those supporting us – our teammates, coaches – are most helpful when they don't criticize or punish us for the mistakes we make when we're still learning the game. Right?

For kids to learn the game of life, they need to have their own experiences, learn their own lessons, and yes, make their own mistakes.

We can best help our kids learn how to live fulfilling, successful lives by accepting their occasional missteps as necessary and important to learning how to play the game.

Encouraging kids to learn from their mistakes enhances their growth. Whereas, punishing, labeling, criticizing, and blaming, shut down the learning process.

Holding fast to the belief that experience and mistakes are good, useful learning opportunities, make us vital members of our children's success teams.

As a child, I had a favorite aunt, Linda, whose nickname for me was "Rookie." I was too young to know what a rookie was, but I liked it because it sounded strong and felt special.

Now that I'm older and know that a rookie is someone who is new something, I can look back and see how Aunt Linda, *treated* me like a rookie, also – with all the respect and forgiveness-of-sins that a great mentor would have for a trainee.

When she spoke to me, I felt like a person, not like a "kid." She never raised her voice, or spoke down to me. She talked to me like a young woman, even at the age of 5.

She treated me like such an equal, that once, when I was 7, I lost my head and talked back to her like she was one of my little friends. She asked me to put away my toys. I didn't want to. I wanted to run outside and play, and put away the toys later.

I rolled my eyes and rotated my neck (the way sassy little black girls did) and answered back, "You ain't my mama."

Whoa!

The look on her face. I can still see it. It wasn't anger. It wasn't, "How dare you, you little brat." It was just... disappointment.

I caught myself in a second. In her eyes, I saw myself fall down rung. After she'd treated me like an adult, I went and acted like a child. I wished I could take it back.

In her same, even tone of voice, she repeated, "Venus, it's time to put away your toys." I quickly answered, "Okay," apologizing with my eyes and tone.

Later, she pulled me aside and told me that what I'd done was "unacceptable." I readily agreed, "I know. I'm sorry." I was relieved by her smile and hug, knowing that the trust I'd broken was restored.

All kids are rookies. They're newbies – little people, learning the game of life.

To really learn, they've got to get involved, try new things, get bumped around a little. They sometimes have to do things wrong in order to figure out how to do things right.

If we come down hard on kids for doing wrong, or "misbehaving," we send the message that mistakes are unacceptable. We shut down the learning process.

Anyone who's new at anything is bound to make mistakes.

We welcome our kids to the game of life and mentor them into adulthood, by respecting their need to play the game and accepting the fact that they will make mistakes.

By encouraging them to explore new things and helping them learn from mistakes instead of punishing them, we keep kids engaged in the game of life. We allow them the hands-on experience they need to develop into the adults they want to be.

The remaining Parenting Tools - 7 - Exploration and Discovery; 8 – Choices; and 9 – Guidance – support our children's need to learn from hands-on experience.

HEART-Based Parenting Approach Toolkit – Tool 7: Exploration and Discovery

Giving our "rookies" a wide playing field will support them in learning what they need to know about themselves and about the world.

There were 2 occasions where I swatted my daughter to try to teach her a lesson. (I hate to say it, but both were prompted by the influence of my well-intended mother.)

The potty training incident you read about earlier was the second occasion. The first was a showdown over compact discs when my daughter was only 11 months old.

My mom was visiting, and making casual comments about my daughter being spoiled.

I felt compelled to prove her wrong.

So, when my daughter crawled over to the CD tower and began sliding out CDs, instead of allowing it and simply putting them back later, like I usually did, I walked over and slapped her hand and firmly said, "No."

It took about 5 times for my daughter to get over the shock, dissolve into tears, and crawl away from the CDs.

After mom left, you can imagine, I felt horrible. I thought, *Now, that's dumb. Kids are naturally curious. If I don't want her to explore something, why not just put it up high where she can't reach?*

I figured if I had to continually swat my kid or yell, "No," to teach her everything that was bad to touch, she might learn to be afraid to explore new things. That can't be healthy for a growing toddler whose mission in life is, "To explore new things."

Exploration

Children are innately curious. They want to know everything about everything. The curiosity that drives them to explore and experiment is healthy. It promotes learning and growth.

Some parents inadvertently squash kids' natural curiosity by not allowing them to explore. Keeping babies safely locked in playpens, or preteens safely locked in the house, limits their freedom to explore and learn about the world around them.

Our fears about danger don't negate a child's need to explore and experiment. There are important things kids can't learn by just watching TV and reading books.

Instead of restricting kids' freedom of movement, it is better to mitigate the dangers as much as possible and teach them how to avoid danger and what to do if something goes wrong.

With toddlers, instead of creating a world of "no" – don't touch this, don't climb on that – we can eliminate as many hazards as possible, so they can safely satisfy their natural curiosity.

Each time their curiosity is rewarded by her learning something new – even if that new lesson involves falling from a non-threatening height – they will grow in confidence and in their ability to tackle life's challenges and discover their power over the world around them.

Discovery

There is a huge difference between *learning* and *being taught*.

"Learning" is active – we're in the driver's seat, we have theories to test and questions to answer. And when we figure out the answer, we really know it. We *own* what we know.

"Being taught" is passive – someone tells us what they think we should know and expects us to remember the info and use it where appropriate. It's not our discovery. We may not remember or understand it. We don't own it.

True knowledge comes through *active* learning. The deepest understanding comes from developing and pursuing answers to our own questions.

We love our kids so much that we want to teach them everything we think they need to know.

However, I've learned from 14 years of homeschooling, that kids learn best when they *discover* the information rather than *receive* it.

You can tell a kid all day long that 2+2=4. He can repeat it, and try to remember it when asked. But when he *figures it out on his own*, when he tests it out with blocks and cars and apples and "discovers" that 2+2 always equals 4, he runs to tell you as if you didn't know. He really gets it. He owns it.

Instead of telling our kids everything, it's better to leave room for them to discover as many of life's truths as they can on their own.

Even *creating opportunities* for them to discover truths is more effective than telling them an important lesson.

For instance, I have a dear friend whose father created an opportunity for her to learn a vital life lesson about empathy when she was a kid, decades ago in the rural south.

Her father overheard her laughing with friends about the plight of the local day-laborers contrasted with their privileged enjoyment of long, lazy summer days.

Rather than lecture her on the virtues of empathy and compassion, my friend's father arranged to drop her off at a cotton plantation for a day so she could experience, first hand, the back-breaking work.

It was one of the pivotal experiences of her life. Through the experience she learned what a lecture could never teach her.

Like me, she is now a family coach, helping other parents to provide active, hands-on growth opportunities for their children. (You can find her at www.todaycoaching.com.)

Here are a few age-appropriate ideas to promote exploration and discovery in your home and support your children's need to learn through hands-on experience.

❖ ❖ ❖ ❖ ❖ ❖ ❖ ❖ ❖ ❖ ❖ ❖ ❖ ❖ ❖

Exercise 8.1: Promoting Exploration and Discovery
   Newborn / Toddlers
1. **Keep Baby in the Action.** Promote your newborn's natural curiosity by carrying her around with you as much as possible. Being mindful of safety, let your baby observe you cooking, talking with friends, gardening. Talk to her about what you're doing. She'll be fascinated, or at least feel included.

2. **Make the House Kid-Friendly.** Put untouchables out of reach. Cover sockets. Lock banned cabinets. Cover furniture and carpets to prevent staining (adhesive runners

are great for carpets). Try to make it so that you never have to say "No" or "Don't."

3. **Do the Switcheroo.** If your kid becomes interested in something you don't want him to explore, offer something different instead. Affirm his curiosity with something like, "Wow, that red thing is interesting, isn't it? Here, check out this red thing." Replace the object of interest and put the "untouchable" away.

School-Aged

1. **Play "Where's the danger?"** The sooner kids learn to scan for possible hazards, the easier it'll be for you to trust that they can explore safely.

    When your kids are playing rough near the coffee table, for example, say, "Pause. OK, where's the danger here? How could you get hurt?"

    When they realize (maybe with a little help at first) that they could hit their heads on the coffee table, ask, "What can you do to make it safer?"

    Let them brainstorm and work out safety strategies – let them move the table, decide to play elsewhere, etc.

2. **Stage "discoveries."** Strategically place educational games and books around the house. Post inspirational quotes and poetry on the walls. Limit television and video game time so that kids look around for opportunities to learn something new.

Teens

1. **Extend boundaries gradually.** Let your teenager prove that she can handle increasing independence a little at a time. For

example, let her go from supervised driving, to taking the car for quick errands, and later to driving friends to a party.

If there's a lapse in responsibility, just go back to a previous independence level, until she shows she can handle it.

2. **Encourage mentors and apprenticeships.** Support your teenager in finding mentors and apprenticing opportunities in their area of interest. Give them a chance to learn, hands-on, what they might like as a hobby or career.

We honor our children's need to learn from experience when we promote exploration and discovery.

We can foster a healthy attitude toward adventure and fun, AND help our kids develop an understanding of what's safe and what's not.

The more kids grow, the more they understand distinctions like "safe vs unsafe," and "good idea vs bad idea." Then they need practice and the freedom to make **Choices** – the next Tool.

HEART-Based Parenting Approach Toolkit – Tool 8: Choices

We all want our young people to make good choices when it counts.

Our teenagers may be asked if they want a cigarette. Our 9 year olds may be tempted to join the schoolyard mob picking on the new kid. Our 5 year olds may want to chase a ball across the street.

We hope and pray that, when the time comes, and we're not around, our kids will choose to do the right thing.

Life is all about choices.

Learning to make good choices takes practice.

Before they face the big decisions that affect their health, safety, and future, we can give them loads of practice making easier choices. We can start offering choices even before they can talk.

It can seem more efficient to tell kids what to do, than to offer choices. It saves time…no drawn out discussions or tedious consequences.

However, barking out fewer commands, and instead, giving kids more opportunities to make choices helps them build "decision-making muscles" – just as letting them walk instead of carrying them all the time builds leg muscles.

The more kids practice making decisions that feel right, the more confident they (and we) become in their decision making skills.

To be sure, there is a time for telling and a time for asking. However, we can give our kids more practice making decisions if we learn to "ask" more than we "tell."

The following ideas can be helpful as we learn to "ask" more and "tell" less. These work with toddlers to teens.

❖ ❖ ❖ ❖ ❖ ❖ ❖ ❖ ❖ ❖ ❖ ❖ ❖ ❖ ❖

Exercise 8.2: Providing More Decision-Making Opportunities

1. **Think: Can I Provide an Option Here?** Become aware of how many things you "tell" your kids to do each day. Turn some of those "telling" instances into "asking" opportunities. You'll find you can give an option without losing any authority.

   When they're very young, like age five and under, it helps to limit choices to two options. For example, "Do you want spinach or broccoli?" Or "We're down to the last book of the night, which would you like me to read, 'Goodnight Moon' or 'Runaway Bunny?'"

   As they get older, let them handle big things like "How would you like to spend our family vacation?"

2. **Follow-Through.** Once your child makes a choice, follow through with it. If, for instance, you've paid for a month of guitar lessons, make sure she understands that she's committed to that month. She make a different choice *after* the paid month is completed.

   This promotes commitment and critical thinking skills. She'll learn to evaluate various options. She'll also learn what it means to take responsibility for one's choices. Over time, she'll confidently own her choices and courageously face the natural consequences.

3. **Asking vs Telling – Know the Distinction.** Only make a request or provide an option when a real choice is available. DO NOT PHRASE COMMANDS AS REQUESTS.

   It is unfair to ask, "Johnny, you wanna buckle your seatbelt now?" if Johnny doesn't have the complete freedom to answer, "No, thank you."

   You can punctuate the command with "please" out of respect and good manners, as in, "Johnny, put on your seatbelt, please." Or you can make the command short and sweet, "Time to buckle up."

   Remember, if the kid isn't allowed to say "no" then there is no choice. Tell, don't ask.

   The exception is when you're limiting the choice to two options and one must be chosen. As in the green vegetable option mentioned above. In this case, make it clear that the only option is one of the proposed items. "No green veggies please," is not an option.

Making choices not only builds "decision-making muscle," it also helps children to develop an internal compass – an inner guide to measure how on track or off course their decisions take them.

They'll rely on this internal compass in the teen and adult years as they navigate everything from peer pressure to consumer advertising to ethical dilemmas.

Looking within to make value-based decisions helps our kids develop sound judgment.

What's the best tool to use when our kids make choices that take them off track?

It's the final tool in our HEART-Based Parenting Toolkit: Guidance.

HEART-Based Parenting Approach Toolkit – Tool 9: Guidance

All of the stories I've shared with you illustrate that *Guidance* trumps *Punishment* as a parenting tool.

Some parenting approaches hold that, to get kids to take the right path, we must punish them each time they take a wrong turn.

Punishment is a POWER tool (it Promotes Obedience While Encouraging Resentment). It contradicts each of the 3 Fundamental Beliefs we've discussed.

In contrast to **the belief that kids are good**, punishment adheres, instead, to the belief that they are bad and must be forced to be good.

Instead of **acknowledging the child as an "unfolding mystery,"** punishment is used to enforce parents' ideas of how quickly children should become what the parents wish them to be.

And, above all, punishment thwarts kids' **need to learn about life through firsthand experience**, by penalizing the mistakes they make as they try to discover for themselves who they are and how to play the game of life.

Guidance, on the other hand, supports all 3 Fundamental Beliefs of the HEART-Based Parenting approach. It shows our kids that we believe they are good, that we trust that they (and we) will ultimately figure out who they are, and that we know they must experience making great and not-so-great decisions in order to grow.

When we guide our kids toward better choices, rather than punishing them for less acceptable ones, we spend more time building them up than tearing them down.

Teaching kids to do right just to avoid punishment trains them to be motivated from the outside in rather than the inside out.

While using guidance instead of punishment gives kids the space to learn to do what's right for its own sake.

Using Guidance to redirect kids to the "right track," means viewing their less productive choices as learning opportunities, rather than crimes.

Following are a few suggestions for practicing the use of Guidance instead of punishment to help kids find the right path.

Exercise 8.3: Using Guidance Instead of Punishment

Newborns – Toddlers

1. **The Fine Art of Distraction.** Divert babies' attention to something they *can* have when what they're asking for can't be given or must wait – instead of punishing the request, which may drive their desires underground.

2. **Model the Use of Language.** When babies grunt and point to tell you what they want, speak their requests while granting them. Encourage them to use more words to get what they want – but don't punish them by withholding things until they say the right thing. Frustration makes learning unnecessarily painful.

School-Aged

1. **Motivate with Empathy.** If your kid breaks a window, takes candy from a store, or does something hurtful to a friend, get her to imagine how the other person feels. Then ask (instead of tell) your kid what she would like to do to fix it. Don't encourage guilt – it's not a healthy motivator – simply teach that we all make mistakes, and most can be fixed.

2. **Teach Reflection.** Getting kids to reflect on the actions they've taken helps them learn valuable lessons. Ask, "What was that like? How'd you like the consequences? Did you get what you wanted? How might you choose differently next time?"

   This helps kids learn to hold themselves accountable, which increases their sense of responsibility.

Teens

1. **Ask, Don't Advise.** Resist the urge to give advice, especially when it's not requested (and even if it is). Show your teen you trust her judgment and resourcefulness by asking instead of telling. Try, "What do _you_ think you should do? What results might you get with that option? What support do you need to make a better decision?"

2. **Let Go Gradually.** Let teens earn greater responsibility and privileges by showing they can handle it a little at a time. For example, if he does well with chaperoned parties for a year, then perhaps allow unchaperoned ones with the caveat that he must observe curfew. If responsibility slips, return to a prior level.

   This is a measured introduction to the freedom of college and adulthood.

Parenting with Guidance instead of Punishment shows our children that we trust them, and see the good in them.

It assures them that their mistakes won't cost them our love.

Guidance, as a parenting tool, assures our kids that we're on their side. Making it more likely that they'll turn to us as valuable team players and coaches in the game of life.

~ CONCLUSION ~

Like the elderly mother who can miraculously lift a fallen car off of her son, all mothers have the power to overcome the weight of a painful history to give our children a chance at a better life.

That's the magical power of love.

Maternal love calls us forth to be the best we can be. It inspires us to draw loving water from what may seem to be an empty well.

The more unconditional love we give to our children, the more we find we can give to ourselves.

That's the healing power of mindful, conscious, empathic, HEART-Based parenting.

Keep these 9 Tools at the top of your parenting toolkit: Empathy, Responsiveness, Closeness, Self-Knowledge, Self-Expression, Loving Communication, Discovery/Exploration, Choices, and Guidance.

Reach for them, and know that you are parenting with HEART: Honesty, Empathy, Appreciation, Respect, and Time.

Let the POWER tools rust away from disuse (those that Promote Obedience While Encouraging Resentment).

Don't lug around useless childhood memories. Either cut them loose, or put them to work.

Let the happy ones remind you of the importance of joy in a child's life – and be a source of that joy for your children.

Let the sad ones remind you of what's hurtful to a child – and take care that your words and actions nurture your children, instead of wounding them.

Forgive your mother for her short-comings as you wish to be forgiven for yours.

Remember, to honor the good that she did, and to learn from the bad.

Become the Mom You Wish You'd Had. Heal yourself and your children. And write a new chapter in your family history.

~ ABOUT THE AUTHOR ~

Venus Taylor is founder of The Family Healing Institute. She is a Certified Family Coach, who studied with some of the most highly regarded family and relationship coaches in the US, including Diana Sterling, of the Academy for Family Coach Training in Albuquerque, NM (www.familycoachtraining.com), and Dr. Susan Campbell, author of *Getting Real,* in Sebastopol, CA (www.susancampbell.com).

She earned her Master of Education from Harvard University with an emphasis on Risk and Prevention.

Venus lives with her husband, Hycel Taylor III, and two children in Boston, MA.

To learn more about her Family Healing programs, visit www.HealMyFamily.com, or email venus@HealMyfamily.com.

Printed in the United States
213216BV00001B/1/P

9 780982 318607